LOUISIANA INDIAN TALES

10.95

LOUISIANA INDIAN TALES

Elizabeth Moore
Alice Couvillon

Illustrated by
Marilyn Rougelot

PELICAN PUBLISHING COMPANY
GRETNA 1990

Library of Congress Cataloging-in-Publication Data

Moore, Elizabeth Butler.
  Louisiana Indian tales / by Elizabeth Butler Moore and Alice
Wilbert Couvillon ; illustrated by Marilyn Carter Rougelot.
      p. cm.
  Summary: A collection of old and new legends about the
Louisiana Indians including "Treasures Under the Earth," "Dark
Moon," and "The Waters of Life."
  ISBN 0-88289-756-X
  1. Indians of North America–Louisiana–Legends. [1. Indians
of North America–Louisiana–Legends.] I. Couvillon, Alice
Wilbert. II. Rougelot, Marilyn Carter, ill. III. Title.
E78.L8M66 1990
[398.2]–dc20   89-71060
                                                          CIP
                                                           AC

Manufactured in the United States of America
Published by Pelican Publishing Company, Inc.
1101 Monroe Street, Gretna, Louisiana 70053

This book is dedicated to our parents, our husbands, and our children—Joseph, Sean, Patrick, Jefferson, Miriam, and Sarah Moore; Caroline, Meg, Emily, and Ginny Couvillon—with love, and to a special friend, Joseph Carpenter.

MANY MOONS

Moon of Fire
Moon of Cold
Moon That Has Watched
My People of Old

Moon of Fire
Moon of Green Corn
Moon That Has Seen
Generations Be Born

Moon of Fire
Moon of Frost
Moon That Has Known
What Memories Have Lost.

Contents

"Legend does not contradict history.
It preserves the fundamental matter
but magnifies and embellishes it."

ADRIEN ROUQUETTE

Acknowledgments

In 1985, we participated with our children in a Louisiana heritage week at Camp Sunshine, a Girl Scout day camp in Fontainebleau State Park in Mandeville, Louisiana. A special day honored the Louisiana Indians, and we realized how little we knew about our own state's Native Americans. We began researching the Tchefuncte, the Choctaw, and the Chitimacha Indians and an exciting and fascinating world was opened. Often, it was difficult finding information on the different periods of the Louisiana Indians, but we enlisted the help of many experts who guided us in this project.

We would especially like to acknowledge Reverend Dominic Braud, O.S.B., whose archaeological findings of Louisiana prehistoric Indians inspired and enlightened us. We truly appreciate his generosity in letting us reproduce in this book the music to "Nature's Praise" and "Zozo Mokeur." His guidance and advice for the story "Song of Nature" were invaluable.

Nancy Hawkins, Louisiana staff archaeologist, spent many hours reading our stories and suggesting ideas to add to their authenticity. With this background, stories came to life. Katherine Byrd, state archaeologist, and Duke Rivet, staff archaeologist, also generously gave of their time and expertise.

We would also like to thank Dr. George W. Shannon, Jr., director of the Louisiana State Museum at Shreveport, who advised us on our early stories and gave us the "hands-on" experience of an archaeological dig; Dr. Geoffrey Kimball, Department of Anthropology, Tulane University, who provided us with knowledge of the Coushatta Indian language; and Dr. Hiram Gregory, Northwestern State University, whose suggestions were deeply appreciated.

We particularly wish to express our gratitude for the interest and help of our contemporary Native Americans of Louisiana: Diana Williamson, Chitimacha Tribe, executive director of the Governor's Commission on Indian Affairs; Earl Barbry, Tunica-Biloxi Tribe, chairman; and Tom and Liz John, Coushatta Tribe.

LOUISIANA INDIAN TALES

1

Treasures Under the Earth

Introduction to Prehistoric Indians
Present-Day Louisiana

Dr. Dominique jumped as Richard and Rob threw open the flap and burst into the tent.

"Whoa! Slow down. What's up?" asked Dr. Dominique.

"Look what we found by the old abandoned house." Both boys held up some broken pottery.

Dr. Dominique took one brown curved piece and walked out into the sunlight. "Well, this is truly interesting. Where did you say you found this?"

"By the old brick foundation to that abandoned house. We were fooling around there and saw one piece. Then, we dug in the dirt and found some more under the house," Rob said excitedly.

Dr. Dominique carefully turned the pieces around to catch the last rays of the setting sun. "This is quite a find. What does this design that's incised on the pottery look like to you?"

"A hand?" answered Richard.

"Yes," said Dr. Dominique, "and if you notice, there's an oblong shape in the center of the palm. That represents an eye. And let me see what you have, Rob. What do you think this is?"

"Big teeth and half a smile."

"Good, Rob! These are important symbols of an Indian religion that flourished from A.D. 1000 to A.D. 1600. We call it the Southern Cult. Let's see, this pottery has pieces of ground shell in it that was used to 'temper' the clay, or hold it together and make it more durable. I suspect that this was made by Mississippian Indians in the 1200s. But what really interests me is that we have never found any evidence before to link any Indians here to the Southern Cult."

"Wow!" shouted the boys together. "Let's go back and get some more!"

"No," said Dr. Dominique. "What is there won't go away. Besides, you boys have really jumped the gun in a major way. We're not even supposed to start near that house until tomorrow." Dr. Dominique carefully placed each piece of pottery into a brown paper lunch bag which he labeled. "Let's finish setting up camp, then we'll build a fire and think about dinner. Boys, the purpose of this camping trip is to learn something about archaeology and the Indians who lived here, to have fun, and for me to get to know my neighbors better. So let's start with the last part and not be so formal. How about calling me Ben, okay?"

"Sure, Dr. Ben," the brothers said together.

"Dr. Ben's just fine boys, just fine."

They got the fire started and cooked some hot dogs and beans for supper. "Look at the lightning bugs," said Richard. "We never see these in New Orleans."

"No," replied Dr. Dominique, "mosquito control pretty much wiped out the fireflies with the mosquitoes. But, as you can see, we have both insects here."

"I'll say," Rob agreed as he slapped a big black bug dining on his ankle. "Toss me the mosquito repellent. I wonder what the Indians used to keep off mosquitoes?"

"I think I can answer that," said Dr. Dominique. "They would rub their skin with bear grease. That did the job. It also kept their skin soft. If things got really bad, they'd take clay from a nearby stream or river and plaster their bodies with it."

Richard looked at a lightning bug that was blinking like a displaced star. "Do you think the Indian kids caught lightning bugs and put them in their tipis to watch at night?"

"They may have," chuckled Dr. Dominique, "but in Louisiana Indians didn't live in tipis. They built their dome-shaped homes out of what they had at hand, which was mud, river cane, and palmetto leaves. These shelters were easy to put up and take down, cool in the summer, and could be made relatively airtight in the winter. A skillful weaver could even make the tightly woven palmetto roof waterproof.

"Let's talk a bit about archaeology before we get started on this dig tomorrow. As I said, you're way ahead of the game. And if you've found what I think you have, it is a very important find. I can check my map and see if the area around the old abandoned house is a site scheduled to be excavated. Remember, boys, I brought you here to see a dig in its first stages. Archaeology is a science, a very precise science. Before we touch anything, we must record and photograph that area."

"Uh, that means we shouldn't have picked these pieces up, huh?" Rob asked sheepishly.

"That's right, Rob, but you really didn't know."

As they watched the fire die down, Dr. Dominique began singing some familiar songs in his deep, rich baritone voice. Then he said, "Boys, as an archaeologist, I've spent many nights sleeping under the stars in the same exact places where the Indians camped. At times I've felt strongly bonded to them. And this song shows how I felt on these beautiful Louisiana nights." Dr. Dominique's voice rose above the summer stillness, and his song filled the air.

After the last notes echoed through the night, Dr. Dominique broke the reflective mood. "It's late and we really

NATURE'S PRAISE
A Louisiana Hymn

text & tune: Fr. Dominic Braud, O.S.B.
accomp.: Robert LeBlanc, O.S.B.

1. Praise the Lord, bay-ou and riv-er, surge and de-liv-er splash-es of light.
2. Praise the Lord, fal-con and swal-low, cir-cle and fol-low heav-en's de-sign.

1. Praise the Lord, light-ning and thun-der, roar out the won-der of his great might.
2. Praise the Lord, white-tail by leap-ing, liz-ard by creep-ing fall in-to line.

1. Swamp and wood re-sound with his glo-ry, ech-o the sto-ry of gifts from a-bove.
2. Man and maid your in-struments ringing fill out the singing of na-ture's great choir.

1. Pine and oak, cy-press and hol-ly dance at his fol-ly, sway in his love.
2. Christ the Lord comes with sal-va-tion; all of cre-a-tion glows with his fire.

need to get an early start in the morning. Let's get some sleep."

The smell of frying bacon got Rob and Richard up quickly the next morning.

"Good morning," Dr. Dominique called as the boys walked out into the hazy morning sun. "There's nothing better than breakfast cooked over a campfire." The boys agreed as they ate the delicious eggs and bacon. After cleaning up, they watched as Dr. Dominique packed his supplies. "What are you putting in your backpack, Dr. Ben?"

"I'm getting the essential tools that we'll need at the site. I've packed a camera, some pointed trowels, pencils, a field log, graph paper, a tape measure, a hammer, stakes, string, and a line level. Fill up your water canteens and we'll be ready to go."

Dr. Dominique and the boys climbed into the jeep and bumped their way to the excavation site.

"Let me explain a little bit about these Indians before we get to the site. Today we'll be examining prehistoric Indian remains. Prehistoric means before writing was invented. Indians have lived in Louisiana for a long, long time. Of course, we don't know exactly when the first Indians arrived, but we have been able to determine that some of the things that they have left behind are at least ten thousand years old."

"That's older than the Romans!" exclaimed Rob.

"Even older than the Greeks," Richard added.

Dr. Dominique agreed. "Older than the Egyptians, too. These prehistoric Indians are divided into different groups according to time periods. The oldest group that lived from 10,000 B.C. to 6000 B.C. was called the Paleo-Indian. These Indians were big-game hunters stalking large woolly mammoths and mastodons."

"You mean, there were woolly mammoths in Louisiana?" Rob asked.

"Yes, Rob, Louisiana was a very different place ten thousand years ago. There were many roaming animals and the Indians were always following the great herds. The Paleo-Indians were nomadic; that is, they were constantly on the move searching for food."

"What was the second group of prehistoric Indians?" asked Richard.

"The Meso-Indians, or Archaic Indians, replaced the Paleo-Indian around 6000 B.C. The large game animals that had been the major food supply during the Paleo-Indian period disappeared due to changes in climate. The Archaic Indian was a hunter of smaller game, such as deer and bear, and he depended more on food like berries and nuts that he gathered in the woods. These Indians were also the first people to domesticate or tame the dog."

"Oh, you mean like dog obedience school?" asked Rob. "I took my dog Sandy to that!"

"No, Rob," laughed Dr. Dominique, "not like dog obedience school. Dogs were once wild and dangerous like coyotes and wolves. These Indians were able to train dogs to help them carry their belongings. In fact, they valued dogs so much that some dogs were even buried with their master." Richard and Rob looked at each other in amazement and Dr. Dominique continued. "The Poverty Point culture lasted from 1700 B.C. to 700 B.C. and followed the Meso-Indian era. These Indians were centered in the northeast part of the state but their influence spread even beyond the area we now know as Louisiana."

"What do you mean, Dr. Ben?" asked Rob.

"Well, Indians from other areas often visited this important political and religious center in order to trade goods. Some came from as far away as Alabama, Florida, and South Carolina. After they finished their business, they returned to their own villages and brought with them not only exotic new items, but new ideas as well."

"But, why is it called Poverty Point? Were they poor or something?" asked Richard.

"Oh, no, this was one of the most advanced cultures at this time in North America. The name Poverty Point came much later after the Indians disappeared. We really don't know what the Indians called themselves or their village.

"Well, we're almost to our site. Remember, there were several other prehistoric cultures, one of which was the Tchefuncte, who were the first to make large quantities of pottery. And the Marksville culture was known for its tremendous ceremonial mounds. There were also the Troyville, Coles Creek, and Mississippian cultures. Each prehistoric culture is unique and fascinating to study. You might say that archaeologists are always trying to piece together a giant puzzle of our Indian heritage. Well, let's see what puzzle pieces we find today, boys. Here we are, at the excavation."

Richard and Rob jumped from the jeep and ran to an area where the land had been measured off into grid-squares bordered by strings. "Look at these squares — they are shaped perfectly," Richard said.

"Yes. I told you archaeologists must be meticulous in order to preserve every piece of information. First, we photograph the site and as we dig, we draw the soil changes and artifacts as they are found."

"What do you mean by artifacts, Dr. Ben?" asked Richard.

"Well, objects made or altered by man that we find buried in the ground that do not naturally occur there, like pottery, charcoal, or projectile points. We also look for bones, seeds, claws, and shells, which give us clues as to what the Indians ate. Laboratory analysis of these different finds can give us all kinds of information such as what plants grew around the site, how the site was used, who used it, and whether or not these Indians traded with other groups. You know, from careful study, an archaeologist can even tell whether the people cooked their fish whole or in fillets! Come see, boys. We've already begun excavation over here."

The boys followed Dr. Dominique to a recently excavated pit. "Hey, that's pretty deep. Did you find anything in that hole?" asked Rob.

Dr. Dominique squatted next to the unit. "We found some broken pieces of pottery, a few nut husks and persimmon seeds, and bones from four kinds of fish. Let's get you two started in this far area. We've only gone down about ten centimeters here. Grab a couple of buckets and let me show you what to do. First of all, you don't dig down into the dirt. You take the edge of the trowel and carefully skim each layer like this. You want the whole area to stay on the same level. I brought the string and line level so you can check to see that you're not going too deep in one part. Okay, boys, you do it!" Richard and Rob stepped over the string, knelt in the dirt, and shaved the surface.

"Good! That's the ticket! Now put the dirt in the buckets and we'll see what you have." The three walked over to a large square screen that was framed with wood and suspended from a tripod by four ropes.

"Okay, Rob, you dump your bucket contents onto the screen and push it back and forth to shake the dirt out."

"Hey, this is fun! Dr. Ben, why are all these shells in here?"

"This is called a shell midden, Rob. The Indians ate lots of clams. They also may have used clams for bait to catch other fish and shellfish. We're not exactly sure of the purpose of these middens. Perhaps they piled up shells in this manner so they could dry shrimp on them. The shells are white and would reflect the sun so the shrimp could dry quickly. But the reason we find so many artifacts in a shell midden is that it really was the village garbage dump."

"I never thought I'd be mucking around in a garbage dump!" said Rob.

"Okay, Rob, stop shaking the screen. Ignore the shells and let's see if we have anything here."

Rob ran his fingers through the shells. "Oh here's a small piece of broken pottery, but there's no design on it. What's this, Dr. Ben?" He held up a small curved white object.

"A deer's tooth, Rob, and look, here's a deer's anklebone."

"Dr. Ben, here's a piece of pottery with a design on it!"

"It looks like that, Rob, but it isn't. It's a charred turtle shell."

"What's this shiny black stuff?"

"Charcoal. We'll find lots of charcoal left over from the Indian fires. I think that's about it. We'll put the bone, tooth, and turtle shell in the 'bone bag,' the charcoal in its bag, and the pottery in the 'pottery bag.' Okay, Richard, we'll discard these shells and then it's your turn."

Richard's finds included a garfish scale used as an arrow point, snail shells, pottery, two broken stone projectile points, and lots of charcoal. The brothers walked back and forth filling the buckets and sifting the contents.

"Dr. Ben, what's this?" Rob held up a long tubular object he found while skimming the dirt.

"Hey, that's a bear's bone, the femur. The Indians ate lots of bear and they fried many foods in bear fat. In the summer, they used the liquid fat over herbs like a salad oil."

"Dr. Ben," said Richard, "you told us that you found seeds and fish bones in that other pit. How did you find something so small?"

"If we're looking for something small, we'll take our dirt samples and run them through the window-screen mesh using water to sift out the dirt. And, you know, after hundreds of years, some of these seeds that we find can still sprout and grow!"

"Really?"

"Really. One of my favorite facts concerns an archaeological find in Bat Cave, New Mexico. Archaeologists unearthed popcorn kernels that were 2,000 years old. You know, that popcorn could still be popped!"

"You mean the prehistoric Indians had popcorn? How did they pop it?" asked Richard.

"In the microwave, of course!" teased Rob.

They all laughed and Dr. Dominique continued. "It's a good guess that the Indians were grinding corn of a popcorn variety and one of the kernels fell close to the fire and accidentally popped. Can you imagine how surprised the Indians must have been?"

"Wow, I bet they had a big popcorn party with that discovery," said Richard.

"Dr. Ben, can we see all the things that you found here?"

"Sure, Rob, but we'll have to go back to the lab. Everything has already been bagged and labeled with a special code. For instance, all artifacts found in this particular pit are designated like this." Dr. Dominique took a stick and wrote the code in the dirt. "16 – ST – 300, Unit N2E2 level 1, pottery bag, Dr. Dominique, 6-9-89."

"What does all this mean?" asked Richard.

"In archaeologists' language, 16 stands for Louisiana, and ST are the initials for St. Tammany Parish. We've named this site the 300th site found in St. Tammany Parish and this is the ceramic contents of the first level of the first excavation unit."

"How did the archaeologists know to dig here, anyway?" Rob questioned.

"The people who recently purchased this property were planting a big vegetable garden. As they plowed up the land, they discovered these potsherds I was talking about and became interested in the possibility that Indians once lived here. Fortunately for us, they acted responsibly and contacted the State Archaeologist/Division of Archaeology in Baton Rouge. She notified me and we got permission to excavate from the property owners."

Dr. Dominique looked at his watch. "Boys, are you getting hungry? Let's head back to our camp and make some peanut butter and jelly sandwiches."

"Great! And you won't have to remind us to wash our hands first!" Richard and Rob held up four extremely dirty hands. The brothers got back into the jeep and Dr. Dominique started the engine.

"Dr. Ben, how did you ever get to be an archaeologist anyway?"

"It's an interesting story. I guess when I was about your age, my dad would take me camping. One day when I was fishing in the river, I discovered three 'arrowheads' in some shallow water. I picked them up and showed my dad. We both knew the Indians made them. We continued to find these 'arrowheads' in the woods and alongside rivers, and soon I had quite a collection. I started to notice that they were not alike, and I was able to put them into groups. One day when I showed them to my class at school, my teacher surprised me when she said that they weren't arrowheads at all!"

"They weren't arrowheads? What were they?"

"They were projectile points. Most prehistoric Indians in Louisiana didn't even know about bows and arrows until after A.D. 1000. They hunted with spear-throwers and projectiles with these sharp points mounted on the end. After that, I began to read whatever I could find in the library on the subject and I've been hooked ever since. I studied archaeology during my four years in college, then got my doctoral degree after eleven more years of graduate school and field work."

Richard said, "We're really sorry about yesterday when we picked up those pieces of pottery. We didn't realize then how important it was to leave everything undisturbed."

"But now you know to protect these sites because, in doing so, you're preserving the record of the people who contributed so much to the heritage of our state." Dr. Dominique pulled up to the campground and smiled at his two friends who were still sitting in the back of the jeep.

"Dr. Ben, this is great! It's the best camping trip we've ever been on!" Richard exclaimed. "I can't wait until we get back to that old house and do things right this time. It's so exciting when you really find something neat!"

Dr. Dominique nodded agreement and reflected, "Richard, Rob, I've been at this for almost twenty years now. But, you know, everytime I find one of these treasures under the earth, I still feel like that little boy who once discovered those three points shining under the water many years ago."

2

The Howling Moon

Archaic Indians, 6000 B.C.–2000 B.C.
La Salle Parish, Catahoula Lake Area

Sula shivered in the crisp night air as she listened to the howling of the wild dogs. Sula hated the night. She felt so small and alone on the scratchy pine-needle mound her mother had fashioned into a bed. Her family slept in a circle around a smoldering fire. Her feet were always too warm, and the fox skins thrown on her body were never enough to keep out the chill night air. Sula covered her ears to block out the sound of the dogs. Some of the older members of the tribe said that the souls of the evil ones dwelled within the wild dogs and caused them to howl at the moon. And stories were told that when the moon glowed in its full circle, it howled back at them.

All of the tribal members despised the dogs. Their hides were not worth curing, and they stole the meat of birds and animals of the hunters. Sometimes, the boys would chase the dogs with rocks and sticks, but even the bravest ran when a dog bared its long, white teeth and growled at them with a hideous grin.

Finally, Sula fell into a restless sleep only to be awakened at dawn by the sounds of the people cooking their morning meal. Sula's mother, Susheena, was heating a small amount

of water in a skin stretched over a forked limb. She mixed in some crushed hickory nuts and some of the last of their grain from grasses that they had gathered on their long march the previous day. After the gruel had cooked, the family dipped their fingers in it and ate what they needed. Sula dried her hands on her hide skirt. She rinsed her fingers in some stored water and ran them through her tangled dark hair.

Sula's people were on the move each season, searching for food. This particular camp, along a large lake her people called "Sacred Lake," was Sula's favorite, especially in the spring. Her chore on this day was to gather the delicious freshwater lotus seeds, wild asparagus, and delicate young shoots that grew along the water's edge. She carefully collected these in a crude leather pouch that Susheena had made for her.

In the distance, Sula watched as a pack of thirsty dogs drank the cool lake waters. They reminded her of the mother dog that had stolen some fresh fish from the camp that morning. She shuddered at the thought of the dog's frantic yelps as it was clubbed to death. The boys had dragged the body off and left it for the vultures.

When she was sure that the dog pack was deep in the woods, Sula scurried to a thicket of trees where rare medicinal fungi often grew around the moist roots. Susheena would dry the fungi and grind it to a fine powder. When anyone had a bleeding wound, she would sprinkle this powder over the cut, and would stop the bleeding with spiders' webs. The wound healed quickly and cleanly, and Susheena was known for her skill and knowledge as a medicine woman.

As Sula probed the pungent earth, she heard a tiny, whimpering sound. She pulled aside some vines and saw two small brown puppies huddled together in a circle of packed dry grass. One hiccoughed silently and the other squeaked at this disturbance. Sula took her finger and rubbed their soft fur. She had never touched a dog before, but these were so small and harmless. She had been warned many times never to go near the young of any animal, because of the concern of the mother, but these puppies had the same marks and coloring of the dog killed at the camp. Surely, they were her pups.

As she stroked one of the puppies, he opened up his bright black eyes and looked at her. He stretched out his two front paws and opened his mouth in a tremendous yawn. Sula picked him up and held him close to her face. He was so tiny and warm and soft. She put his full warm belly against her cheek and smelled his sweet puppy smell. The other puppy squirmed and whimpered as she tried to find her warm brother. Sula picked her up with her left hand and held both pups. They wiggled as she lay them down on their grassy nest and they lumped back together in a little mound. Sula lay down close to them and petted their glistening brown fur. The pups snuggled up close to her and fell asleep. The sun warmed Sula's golden skin. She felt her eyes get heavy and was soon as sound asleep as the pups.

Sula woke up to whimpering sounds. The little pups were hungry and were sniffing around for their mother. Sula carried a little pouch with strips of dried deer meat. She chewed some of the meat until it was soft, spread it on her fingers, and watched as the puppies eagerly licked every morsel. Sula continued feeding the babies until all of the meat was gone.

As the sun was starting to dip low in the sky, Sula knew it was time to pick up what she had gathered and start home. The pups watched her closely with their big, black eyes. Sula was confused and worried. She dare not bring the hated dogs back to the tribe, but she knew it was certain death for the little dogs if she left them alone. As Sula turned to leave, one pup stood up on wobbly legs and rolled over with a squeal as it tried to follow her. Sula threw out the gathered food, scooped up the pups, and put them in her carrying pouch.

Susheena was watching for Sula as she slowly returned to the family fire. "I see why you are so late in returning. Your pouch is full and heavy so you must have found many seeds and herbs."

Sula lowered her eyes as she gently placed the pouch on the dirt. Susheena reached into the pouch and screamed as she felt not seeds and shoots but something alive and furry. Other families came running over at the cries of distress. Everyone stopped in angry disbelief when the two puppies stumbled out. Sula hung her head lower and a tear trickled down her cheek.

When her mother could speak again, she said in a quiet voice, "Why have you done this, my daughter?"

As Sula held back her tears and tried to speak, one of the puppies wobbled to Susheena's fingers and began licking them with little whimpering cries.

An older boy roughly grabbed the baby dog and tossed it to his friends. "You take this one and I'll grab the other. We'll see how far we can throw them! That will be the end of these messy things!"

Sula's face was wet with tears as she gasped with short, choking sobs.

"Stop!" said Susheena to the boys. "Put them down now!" Susheena had much status and the boys obeyed immediately. They turned away angry and ashamed, and the rest of the tribe went back to their fires, talking in whispers about the unwanted additions to their group.

After the sun had come and gone five times, Sula's friends started to stop by and pet and play with the puppies. The elders did not like the situation, but they did not want to anger Susheena. One of Sula's friends was a boy named Caho. Caho came often to play with the pups and to feed them. Sula soon realized it would be hard to take care of both puppies and also keep up with her chores, so she gave one to a delighted Caho. She kept the other and named him Hoyo, which meant "red eyes."

Hoyo grew big and strong and always stayed by Sula when she went out to gather food. She was never lonely with Hoyo, and she talked to him the same way she spoke with her friends. He would cock his head and lift up his ears to listen. Susheena was happy that Hoyo stayed by Sula, for Hoyo would growl if he sensed danger from a snake, and once he chased away a red wolf that scared Sula. The other tribal members noticed this too and looked forward to both dogs visiting their family fires to beg tasty morsels of food. Even the two older boys would throw sticks for the dogs to fetch back to them.

One day, Sula was probing the ground with her pointed stick. She came across a large number of a favorite root. She loaded the pouch until it was full. She was sorry that she was so far away and could carry no more of her plentiful find. Suddenly, it occurred to her that the pouch handle could fit around Hoyo's neck so that the heavy roots were supported on either side of his back. Now, she was able to carry more roots in her skirt. Susheena laughed when she saw Hoyo trotting back to camp with his burden. "Hoyo, what a clever dog you are! You can do the work of a big boy now!" Others gathered to see this strange sight, and Hoyo walked proudly around, enjoying the extra attention.

Susheena and the tribe soon realized what a wonderful help a dog could be. Susheena thought more about this strange idea of a dog carrying things and tried many ways to make it easier for Hoyo. She fashioned a harness out of deer sinew and attached two long poles to each side of the harness. She wove a loose, flat basket between the poles. Hoyo could then drag heavier and longer items that were placed in the basket. The next time the tribe moved to another campground, all were amazed to see how much Hoyo could help. Hoyo was happy too because he got many fond pats on the head and special treats. A new set of carrying poles were made for Caho's dog too.

That night beside the fire, Sula hugged Hoyo. She was no longer afraid of the night because Hoyo was her friend who would help and protect her. And she was no longer cold, because Hoyo would snuggle up to her and keep her warm throughout the whole night.

3

The City of the Sun

Poverty Point Indians, 1700 B.C.–700 B.C.
West Carroll Parish, Epps

The sun split into long rays as it shone through the trees. Modoc shaded his eyes with his hand as he looked up from the forest floor. The air was heavy with the spicy scent of pine, and the squirrels chattered as they threw down pinecone cobs after they had finished eating the fresh green petals. The fallen leaves that padded the ground were releasing the moisture from early morning dew, and Modoc walked through a steamy mist.

He came to a clearing and flung out his arms as he let the sun fall upon his golden skin. The warmth penetrated his body, and he felt invigorated and refreshed. He started out again in a loping trot in the direction of his uncle's house. He was going to stay with his mother's youngest brother for a full cycle of the moon. While there, he would sharpen his hunting skills in the manner of the men of the tribe. He always enjoyed his stays with his uncle, Lothog. He was glad for a vacation from the hubbub of his home. Modoc's older sister, Alita, was always telling him what to do and how to do it. He got along well with his younger twin brothers, Ganok and Sholto, but they were like his double shadows.

Everywhere he went, they wanted to go. Whatever he did, they tried to do. It was nice to be so admired, but sometimes it got to be annoying. Modoc had to smile when he thought of the twins. They looked so much alike that only the family could tell them apart, and they were constantly playing jokes on their teachers by changing places on them. Ganok and Sholto were so good-natured that no one could get really angry with them. The twins were special to the tribe, and were considered a sign of favor from the gods. They were carefully taught at a very young age to develop the talent of prophecy that twins were thought to have.

Modoc arrived at Lothog's village, which was beyond the City of the Sun. His uncle had recently married, and he and his wife lived in a small hut. Lothog was out in front preparing the game for the evening meal, and when Modoc appeared the two relatives greeted each other warmly. Modoc helped skin and dress the animals.

After they had eaten, a neighbor, Alana, dropped by and asked Modoc to come out and play. Modoc gruffly replied that he had no more time for such childish activities. Alana only smiled at his rudeness and gracefully walked out. Modoc was surprised at how pretty Alana had become. She looked the same, but she was different too. It confused him and made him uncomfortable.

The next day Modoc got reacquainted with the boys of the village. He was delighted to hear that a stickball game was scheduled for late that afternoon. Stickball was a very serious game for the tribal adults. It was the way to settle arguments and disputes. The young boys were carefully trained in the game, for it would be valuable to them when they grew up.

The boys all gathered at the appointed time and two priests held up straws. The hidden tips of the straws were dyed red and blue to determine the two teams. Modoc pulled a red straw. Modoc was a valued teammate, for he was a very swift runner.

The two priests said prayers over the teams, then took the sharp fang of a rattlesnake and made tiny scratches on the boys' legs to instill the striking power of the reptile. The players were all given two sticks with squirrel-skin nets attached to the ends. Each team tried to throw a leather ball with the nets to the other team's goal.

Modoc and his Red Team played fiercely, but the teams were evenly matched and neither side could gain many points. It was a spirited game and the onlookers cheered with loud songs for their favorite team. Once Modoc glanced over to the gathering crowds and saw Alana watching him. His cheeks glowed and he turned back to his game with greater determination. At the moment of sunset, Modoc's team was ahead by two points. Lothog ran up and clapped Modoc on the shoulder, for he was proud that his nephew had played so well and helped the Red Team win.

The game had been exciting, and it was hard to settle down. Modoc knew, though, that he had to sleep because in the morning his instruction would begin. His uncle was well known for his skills in making tools and weapons, and Modoc was eager to practice under his watchful eyes.

The process of making stone points had been perfected through generations. Lothog showed Modoc how to give a piece of flint rock a hard blow in order to obtain a flake with which to work. With the smaller piece, Modoc learned to apply pressure with a deer antler to chip away tiny bits of rock until he had a perfect point. Flint knapping did not take a great deal of time, but Modoc had to develop a skill of looking at a rock and recognizing the best place to make the initial blow. Flint rock came from distant lands and no part was wasted. Modoc saved all of the chips to make tiny drills and scrapers.

After he had a pouch full of spear points, Lothog gave him a lesson in the construction of an atlatl, a throwing stick essential in killing the swift white-tailed deer. The spear was hooked onto the atlatl, and with a smooth, arcing motion, the hunter, holding onto the stick, would release the spear which flew toward the target. Modoc gathered straight pieces of light cane and, with deer sinew his uncle gave him, tied his spear points onto the cane. Then, he and Lothog went out to the field to begin hours and hours of practice to gain accuracy and strength.

At the end of the month, it was time to return to the City of the Sun. It was not a long journey, but Lothog and Modoc left before daybreak, travelling in the cool morning hours in order to escape the intense heat of the day. Even before sunrise, there were many others making their way to the City of the Sun. The Festival of Light, the most important ceremony of the year, was to begin tomorrow and people from all the outlying villages came to the ceremonial center.

From miles away, Modoc could see the City of the Sun. The site was constructed on six semicircular ridges that had been built up ten feet above the flat ground. Six thousand people lived and worked together on these ridges. The center of the city was a huge mound, one hundred feet high. Shaped like a flying bird, this was the sacred pulse of the people. At sunrise, everyone would gather at the base of the mound on the day when the sun stood highest in the sky, and the rejoicing and celebrating would begin.

Modoc was happy to see his family again. He was even glad to see Alita! The twins were delighted to have not only their older brother back, but their favorite uncle too. After the family greeted each other, the preparations for the festival began. The women had already made balls of clay mixed with sand. These were molded by hand into different shapes and fired until hard. These balls would be dropped into a pit of hot ashes during cooking. They maintained the heat of the fire and cooked their food. Alita and her mother wrapped raw pieces of rabbit and deer in large palmetto leaves and placed them in the pit when the clay balls glowed.

While the meat cooked and the aroma filled the air, the women ground wild rice and pecans and mixed this with mushrooms that had been gathered and dried. Some of the men left to hunt, while others tried their skill at fishing. Modoc and the twins went down to the bayou to check the cane fish traps and to set a hook line for the night. Modoc was upstream working with the hooks, and Ganok and Sholto were checking individual traps when Ganok turned and saw a log slowly floating against the current toward him. He screamed when he saw two bumps of eyes protruding from, not a log, but a hungry alligator! Sholto scrambled out of the water, but Ganok tripped on the slippery grass which tangled around his foot.

Modoc realized what was happening and raced through the water towards Ganok. Many thoughts went through Modoc's mind as he sprinted toward his struggling brother. He had watched his father and uncle catch alligators many times and Lothog had even let Modoc capture a baby alligator after careful instruction and under watchful eyes. But this alligator was not a baby, and if Modoc did not do something fast, his brother would die at the jaws of the reptile.

The alligator was so intent on the flailing, splashing child, that it was unaware of Modoc's closeness. Modoc quickly curled his fingers around the long bottom jawbone and clamped his thumbs on top of the reptile's snout. Before the beast's slow brain registered what was happening, Modoc mounted the alligator and wrapped his legs around the base of its thick tail. When Modoc edged his thumbs up to shut off the alligator's nostrils, the creature reacted violently. He furiously whipped his tail around, and started turning over and over to get rid of his unwelcome passenger. The water splashed and foamed as Modoc held on with all his strength.

Sholto freed Ganok from the grasses and the twins raced toward the village for help. Modoc gritted his teeth and grimly held on. He knew that the alligator had a reserve air supply in little pockets behind his ears and that it could fight for a long time without fresh air. The battle was not one of brute strength, but whether the boy or the reptile could hold out the longest. Modoc's fingers were white as he squeezed the jaws together and his legs were tiring being wrapped so tightly around the tail. If he weakened and let go, the powerful creature would kill him with one clamp of his tooth-lined jaws.

Modoc was trembling with fatigue when Lothog, armed with a spear, raced to the water. Just as Lothog started to grab the alligator's jaws to help the boy, he hesitated. He saw the look of determination in Modoc's eyes, and he realized that the flailings of the alligator were getting slower and slower. Modoc also felt the reptile weakening, and carefully rolling the alligator on its back, he slipped off. Modoc's fingers were still locked around the alligator's jaws, and with his last bit of strength, he pulled the limp creature onto the grassy shoreline. Lothog looked at Modoc and quietly handed him the spear. Modoc lifted it high, and plunged the sharp stone point into the soft white throat of the reptile.

The monster was dead. Modoc stared at the alligator's powerful jaws and spiny pointed tail, suddenly understanding his great accomplishment. He was now a man; he had known no fear against his enemy. His courage was immense. With Lothog's help, he dragged the alligator back to his home. Many, who had gathered to watch the procession, congratulated him on his great ability. But no one was prouder than his parents. His mother held him close. His father beamed and praised his skill as a hunter. Lothog handed Modoc the bloody spear. It had been one that Modoc had made. It, too, had passed the test.

Lothog lifted Ganok onto his shoulders and the family danced around the still reptile. Soon neighbors and friends joined in the excitement. Modoc, jumping on the dead alligator's back, re-enacted the drama at the bayou while everyone cheered and clapped. The atmosphere was charged with the excitement of the hunt and festival which was to begin shortly.

Before daybreak on the Festival of Light all the hearth fires were dampened and put out. Modoc could not remember it ever being so dark. All the tribal members gathered at the base of the Sacred Mound. The chief stood at the very top of the mound and held his arms high over his head, facing the direction of the sunrise. The sun burst over the horizon and bathed the city and its people in a golden light. The chief turned and swung his arms in a long arc indicating which direction the sun would take.

At an altar on the mound's base the holy priest knelt as he began to kindle a fire. He positioned a stick on a flat bark on which dry lichens and moss were scattered. He twirled the stick between his palms, and the crowd cheered as the moss flamed up and the first puffs of smoke appeared. Then the priest took a long torch and lit it. The crowd was suddenly quiet, anticipating the moment of his long-awaited announcement.

The highest honor that could be given to a member of the tribe was to deliver the sacred fire to the top of the mound where ordinarily only the chief and the priest could walk. This honor was given at the Festival of Light to the one who had shown the most courage during the year. The priest pointed the torch to the sun and in a loud voice cried out Modoc's name.

Again the crowd cheered and they parted as Modoc made his way to the altar. He knelt in front of the priest and lowered his head. The priest then took the sacred rock that was being warmed by the full rays of the sun. One side of the rock had been skillfully angled and highly polished. The priest approached Modoc and held the rock in such a position that sunbeams were reflected off the rock and onto his head. With this gesture the priest instilled in Modoc the everlasting power and light of the sun.

Modoc received the burning torch, slowly climbed the steps to the top of the mound, and re-lit the sacred fire that would burn for the entire year. Looking down on the crowd, he was able to pick out his family and friends. As he gazed on their upturned faces, he understood that the honor bestowed on him reflected on his family as the rays of the sun reflected off the sacred rock. He closed his eyes and turned his face full to the sun. The warmth penetrated his eyelids as a burnished light filled his being, and he became one with the sun.

4

The Gift of the River

Tchefuncte Indians, 500 B.C.–A.D. 400
St. Tammany Parish, Covington

Natal was the first to greet the new day in the season of autumn. Large persimmons hung like lanterns from the trees as he walked the trail to the river. He stopped at the bluff overlooking the amber water. Natal froze as he saw three deer, their images ghost-like in the morning mist. They scampered away when he tried to come closer.

The river provided many gifts for Natal's family. They fished in it and caught bass, catfish, and beautiful sunfish that had bright bellies like the setting sun. Calcaso, his father, hunted the beavers that built dams along the river, and his family used the beavers' pelts to make clothes in the winter and keep their dwelling place warm.

Natal's trip down to the river was fun. He tossed his mother's water bags on the sandy river bank and slid down the slippery clay bluff. Going back with heavy waterskins, though, was a hard job. But he had to hurry to his mother, Katlaha, so that she could begin preparing a morning meal. Natal was eager for the day to start, for today Calcaso had promised to take him along for the hunt.

His mother and younger sister, Tala, were just coming out of their palmetto hut when he returned. Katlaha took the

water to mix with parched acorn meal and the family ate the porridge with wooden spoons.

When they had finished, Natal gathered everything he needed for the hunt with his father. Now that he was getting bigger, he was becoming skilled with the blowgun. He had learned to make it from a long piece of hollow river cane. The darts were sharpened pieces of wood with thistledown tied to them to make them fly. Natal would put a dart in his blowgun, aim at a squirrel, give a mighty blow, and hope to have roasted squirrel for his next meal.

It would soon be time for him to hunt with an atlatl and spear like his father. He had already learned to make spearpoints by carefully chipping away flakes of rock with a smooth, rounded stone. And he was especially proud the day when his father selected one of his points to hunt a wild bear!

While the men hunted, Katlaha and Tala joined the other women by the river. They spoke excitedly as they wove baskets of all shapes and sizes.

"Why is everyone so busy?" Tala asked.

"Oh, Tala," her mother answered, "we didn't tell you. There is a wedding at the village near the Wide Lake. It is a time of celebration, but there is much to do. The men must hunt food for our journey, and we will bring these baskets for gifts."

"Teach me to make a basket so that I may give a gift, too," Tala said.

"You are still too young, my child, but, why don't you make something pretty out of the river clay and bring it as your special gift?" Katlaha asked.

"That will be fun. I will make it now." Tala knelt down on the sand and scooped the white clay from the shallow river. She returned to her mother's side and began playing with the clay. She rolled it in her palms until it was a nice, round ball. Then, she stuck her thumb down into the center of the ball and made a tiny bowl. Tala took another piece of clay and rolled it with her fingers until it was a long, skinny snake. She made another snake and coiled it around and around to look like some of the snakes she had seen sleeping in the hollow logs. "Look, Mother," Tala squealed, "look at the pretty things I made."

Katlaha held the tiny clay pieces and beamed. "These will be perfect wedding gifts. Now, come, we have finished our baskets and must return to our village. The men will be coming home soon, and we must have the fires ready to smoke and dry the meat."

Tala carefully placed her clay objects on a piece of flat pine bark and followed her mother. She watched as the women cut fresh green twigs from the trees and asked, "What are the branches for, Mother?"

"The fresh wood we will add to the fire pit to make smoke to cure the meat," Katlaha explained. "Could you help us gather some twigs?"

Tala picked some small branches and added them to her piece of pine bark. She was proud to be able to help.

When the women arrived at the campsite, they began readying the fire. In a large pit, dug deep into the ground, the women added dried wood to the blackened, charred remains of previous fires. The men returned after a successful hunt. The wild turkeys and rabbits were prepared by the women and roasted over an open fire. While the women cooked, the men bowed reverently over the slain deer, thanking it for the food it provided. Then, they skinned the animal and cut strips of meat.

The pit was ready with glowing charcoal. "Tala, bring your green wood now and throw it into the fire," Katlaha called.

Tala tossed the bundle of sticks and then cried out in horror, "My gifts, my gifts! My clay snakes and bowl are in the fire. Get them out before they burn!"

"Oh, Tala, we cannot get them out. The fire is too hot," her mother sighed.

Tala sobbed as Natal approached. "I will bring you to the river, Tala. You can make some more."

When the two walked away, Katlaha placed the raw deer meat on a rack of fresh twigs and lowered it into the burning pit. Wet Spanish moss covered the opening and a delicious smell filled the air.

The family packed the next morning and started on their long walk. When they arrived at the Wide Lake, they were happy to see their relatives and friends. All day the Indians talked, and traded goods, and prepared for the feast that night. Natal and Tala met up with their friends and soon had several games going. While the women were preparing the deer and bear for the meal that evening, the children took the deer bladders, washed them, and blew them up like balloons and batted them around. The older boys found some small, round water-smoothed hearts of pine that they knocked along the sand with sticks.

That night there was a great feast with roasted meat, steamed oysters, and dried shrimp. After everyone had eaten his fill, some of the musicians of the tribe got out their drums. The young adults danced, and the older people watched, and clapped, and sang.

The wedding was the next day, and after much merriment, Calcaso's family headed back to the river. When they arrived, Tala asked her mother, "Do you think the fire is cold now? May I get my snakes and bowl?"

Her mother said, "Tala, the fire was so hot and lasted so long that your clay burned to ashes. Do not be disappointed."

"Well, I will still check the pit." With a long stick, Tala stirred the cold ashes. Her stick hit a hard object. She was amazed to see one of her skinny snakes in the remains of the fire.

"Natal, Natal, come see!" she cried.

Natal ran to his sister.

"Natal, come get my snake out of the cold ashes. It did not burn up."

Natal reached down into the pit and pulled up the long, skinny snake which now was as black as his sooty fingers. He turned it around in the palm of his hand and wondered what magic had caused it to become so hard and strong. He took the stick and found the tiny clay bowl and coiled snake too.

Tala was filled with surprise, and she ran to show her mother.

"What is this that you give me?" Katlaha asked, holding the small objects. Then she understood that these were the clay gifts that had fallen into the fire and become hard. When she tapped them together, there was a clicking sound. It was a mystery.

"Let's go to the river and wash off the black soot," Tala said, pulling at her mother's arm.

At the river, Katlaha scrubbed and scrubbed, but the black color remained. Surprisingly, the clay did not soften. The tiny bowl held water and did not leak. Katlaha turned the hard clay pieces over in her hands, wondering if this were some gift from their god.

Katlaha was so fascinated with this discovery that she and Tala made many clay bowls of different sizes, built a new fire, and placed the bowls into the hot fire pit. Again, they covered the fire with wet moss. The fire burned all day and night and into the next day. When the ashes were cold, Katlaha removed the moss. Tala jumped up and down and clapped her hands when she saw that again the clay had turned into hard, blackened bowls.

When Katlaha and Tala had made and baked many bowls, they sent a messenger to gather the neighboring Indians to the banks of their amber river. The tribal members were told only that Calcaso's family wanted to show them a special gift of the river.

When everyone arrived, they were amazed to see the clay bowls holding water and being used for cooking vessels. Katlaha and Tala shared all they knew about how the bowls were made. The women of the tribe watched and learned. And from that time on, Calcaso's family was held in great honor.

From generation to generation, as the moon of fire changed to the moon of frost, Indian families gathered in their homes on cool, autumn evenings. The father would light his pipe and tell his sleepy children the well-loved story of the river god's gift to their tribe.

5

Dark Moon

Houma Indians, Late 1600s
Terrebonne Parish

Taina's heart thumped in her chest and her breath came in quick gasps. The Spirit Man had announced that there would be a special sign from the moon tonight. All had come together to chant and pray. The drummers beat rhythmic tones on their cypress knee drums, and the dancers shuffled in a circle and shook their turtle-shell rattles at the sky.

The drummers ceased their throbbing rhythms as the dancers dropped to their knees. The silence was broken by the haunting wails of the reed flutes. All eyes were on the moon as a veil was drawn across its face. The moon darkened, and was circled with a halo of dull orange fire. The flute sounds drifted off, and the Spirit Man stood in the middle of the dancers. He lifted his hands to the sky and cried out in a loud voice, "Oh, Dark Moon! You hide your face from us. We beat our chests and weep bitter tears. We are enclosed in a cycle of trouble and woe. Our enemies cross our sacred boundaries to hunt in our land and our own people go hungry. I will go into the forest, to the womb of the Earth Mother, to fast and pray during three risings of the sun so I may dream the vision of your desires. Oh moon, light of the night, smile down upon your children once again." Taina's dark eyes glowed as she watched the moon slowly begin to shed its light once again. The drums sounded and the dancers' feet circled once more in the ancient steps.

The Spirit Man retreated to the woods and Taina wondered what the message of the moon would be. She looked again at the sky and sighed with relief when she saw that the moon was whole once again and shone with a dull silver light.

Taina was very tall for a young woman, taller than most of the men. She was a classic beauty of the Houma tribe. Her limbs were long and slender and finely drawn. Her moist black eyes glistened in her full round face. She had high cheekbones, and her skin was a vibrant copper color. Her hair was black but when the sun shone full upon her, it tipped her hair with glints of red fire. She could outrun the boys her age, taking big strides with her long straight legs. She was skilled in hunting with the blowgun and bow and arrow, and her athletic prowess made her a valuable team member for any game.

Three days later, when the Spirit Man had returned from his vision quest, the people prepared for a special midnight ceremony. They placed large river stones in a circle on the earth, and crossed the circle with other stones in the line of the four directions. Flags of dyed deerskin were thrust in the ground—the white flag to the north, red to the east, yellow to the south, and black to the west. All the people, even the smallest children, placed their own small stones outside the circle. When everything was ready and the moon was high in the sky, musicians and chanters played and sang, and the dancers marched in the sacred circle, the Circle of Life. At midnight the Spirit Man walked into their midst, carrying a torch that he had lit from the perpetual fire that he carefully tended. Logs had been placed in the center of the circle, and as he set his torch among them, they flared up and united in a single flame.

The Spirit Man lifted his face to the sky and chanted a long prayer. Then he turned to the people and said, "Many things have been revealed to me. Tonight I will tell you some of these revelations. No longer will we allow the Bayougoula Indians to cross our boundaries that we have marked with a red stick. They violate our land and snatch the food meant for our children's mouths. We must arm ourselves and prepare for battle. Our guiding moon revealed a message to our people. I have learned in a dream that as the moon has hidden its light from us, we too have a hidden light in our midst. The shadow must be lifted from this light so that it may be known. This light will lead us into battle and victory, and will become great among our people."

The Spirit Man picked up a bowl of cornmeal, walked around the circle, and consecrated it by sprinkling the meal on the stones. He took the sacred calumet, or ceremonial pipe, lit it from the everlasting flame, and watched as the smoke rose, carrying his prayers to the Creator. After the pipe ceremony, he drew forth a bound sheath of sweet grass, and lit it from the perpetual fire, so that it burned with a black smoke.

"Taina, you are that special light. Come forward." Taina rose gracefully and stood before the Spirit Man. He circled around her with the burning grasses so that she was enveloped by the thick black smoke. After the ceremony, Taina and the Spirit Man talked until a pink dawn banished the shadows of the night. The Spirit Man had carefully instructed Taina on how to prepare herself for her great task. She drank the sacred black drink of purification, then cleansed herself in the holy waters of the stream. She donned the special white garments that had been prepared for her, which had been made from the softest doeskin.

Taina hid in the forest, to pray and fast. After several days, she fell into a coma-like sleep, and dreamed visions of her destiny. When she awoke, she returned to the stream and

drank from it, for this holy water was the lifeblood of the
Earth Mother. She felt its healing energy flow through her,
and she went to the Spirit Man and told him what she had
experienced. He reached into his deerskin bag and took out
a small rock disc. He held it in the palm of his hand and Taina
saw that it was a perfectly round stone of a type that she had
never seen before. It was translucent and was the color of the
palest moon. He slipped it into a small pouch, and Taina
lowered her head as he placed it around her neck. "This is
your totem. Never take it off."

When Taina had taken food and rest, she gathered the
tribal warriors and walked to the red post to discuss their
plans. These posts separated the hunting areas of the Houma
and the Bayougoula. The post was taller than the height of
five men and was decorated with designs of fish. The lower
part of the post was covered with skulls of animals and fish
that had been sacrificed. The Spirit Man solemnly placed the
head of a bear on the post, and the talk of a battle plan began.

Taina had selected for her weapon a large club of heart of
pine that had been naturally formed by the action of the
waters of the bayou. The warriors waited for the right night
for their surprise attack. Finally the moon and stars were
covered with clouds and the Houma war party assembled.
They stealthily approached the Bayougoula village. Taina's
voice split the air with a fierce guttural cry, and the attack
was launched.

Both sides fought bravely, and the dirt darkened with
blood. Taina heard a warning cry and whirled around to see
the chief of the Bayougoulas racing towards her armed with
a large stone ax. He thrust it downward, and as she quickly
sidestepped she could hear the wind whistling as the ax flew
by her ear. Before he could raise his ax again, she swung her
club in a wide arc and the chief fell to the earth. When the
Bayougoula warriors saw that their chief was slain, they

threw down their arms and knelt before this woman whom they thought was instilled with supernatural power.

The triumphant Houmas returned with twenty-five prisoners. Taina walked in front of the war party as young men danced and sang and held up calumets. The regal woman stood in front of her people, and the trembling slaves were thrown to the earth before her. They waited in great fear to hear of their fate.

"You have violated a sacred trust and crossed over our boundaries. Never again must this happen. You will take a solemn oath that you will forevermore respect the rights of others. In return, I, Taina, speaking for the great nation of the Houmas, will adopt you as my children. My brothers and sisters are your brothers and sisters. My land is your land. My people are your people—we are one."

The Bayougoula captives could not believe their good fortune. The tribal women wept over them, treated their wounds, and gave them food.

Taina was a strong and wise ruler for many years. She earned the love of her people and the respect of other tribes. And after her death, according to legend, Taina became one of the brightest stars to nestle close to the moon. Her mortal remains were encased in a finely carved shrine which was placed with honor before the perpetual fire, and she was revered in death as she was in life.

6

The Secret
of the Hidden Book

Introduction to Historic Indians
Present-Day Louisiana

"Look out for snakes!" Dr. Dominique called to the boys as
they ran through the tall grass towards the old abandoned
house at their excavation site. "It is really overgrown here—
this is a fine hide-out for a water moccasin. You know we're
not far from the river!" Richard and Rob froze in mid-step
and waited for Dr. Dominique to catch up to them. "Come on
boys—you're not afraid of a little snake are you?"

Rob answered, "No, we're not afraid of little snakes, it's
just the big ones that have us worried!"

"Just be on the lookout. They won't hurt us if we don't
bother them," Dr. Dominique replied.

Soon they spotted the old mossy brick path to the house.
They followed it as it curved around a huge old magnolia tree
and led up to the structure's rotting front steps. "Can we go
inside?" asked Richard.

"Yes," Dr. Dominique replied. "The property's owners are
very anxious to find out all they can about the land and its
previous inhabitants." Dr. Dominique carefully led the way
up the loose boards on the steps, and across the sagging
porch. The door creaked on its hinges as they opened it, and
they stepped into a musty room.

Rob said, "Wow, this house must be a thousand years old!"

"Not quite," Dr. Dominique answered. "It was a fine old house, probably built before the Civil War—maybe 1850 or so. Let's take a look around."

They walked through the four rooms of the house trying to imagine what each room looked like years ago. Rob plopped down on an old chair and sneezed as a large cloud of dust covered him. He pleaded, "Quick! Open a window! Let's get some air in this place."

Richard struggled unsuccessfully to open the big window, and said,"Look at these spider webs—it's like the spiders are trying to make lace curtains for the windows!"

Dr. Dominique laughed, "That must be nature's way of decorating! Let's go back and check out that old desk in the front room. You never know what you might find in the shelves and drawers."

The boys opened each drawer and probed the dusty corners. "There's nothing in here, Dr. Ben. All we found was this old feather," Rob said.

"Let me see, boys. That's not just a feather, that's a quill pen. See how the point has been sharpened and darkened by the ink? I bet you can find a bottle of dried ink in there somewhere if you look." The boys continued their search, opening the tiny drawers and doors at the top of the desk.

"There's a book behind this door!" Rob exclaimed as he pulled it out. "Hey, this book is fake! It's made out of wood and it's hollow inside."

Richard took the book from him and said excitedly, "It's a secret compartment! We found a secret compartment!" Richard turned the "book" over and shook out a faded yellow envelope. He handed it to Dr. Dominique.

"This is very old and fragile. We must handle it carefully or it will tear apart." Dr. Dominique opened the envelope and slipped out a delicate paper.

Richard said, "Look at that writing! It's brown and spidery. I can't read what it says."

Dr. Dominique examined the letter closely. "It's written in French, boys. Look at that date – 1706. This is amazing! A real piece of history!" Dr. Dominique brought the letter over to a shuttered window where a weak light filtered through. His eyes lit up as he started translating the letter: "*Mon cher Papa* – my dear Father – I hope that all is well with you, Mother, Conette, and Celeste. We have suffered a shortage of supplies, and the commander of Fort de la Boulaye, St. Denis, has sent your dear son and eleven other Frenchmen to live among the friendly Acolappissa and Natchitoches Indians on Bayou Castine. It took us a week by boat to reach their village, which consists of twenty bark cabins surrounded by a fence of pointed stakes. On our trip to the village, we killed six deer and eight turkeys, so we were warmly welcomed. The Indians embraced us and we were happy that we had come. They cooked the meat we had provided, and after supper, we danced and sang late into the night. One of our men played the violin and the Indians all laughed when they saw us dancing the minuet together. I must say it was quite a sight!

"I was invited to lodge with the chief of the Natchitoches tribe and I was treated kindly in his home. The morning after our dancing I was greeted by my host carrying a large platter of fish fried in bear fat. We also had sagamité, a type of bread made with cornmeal and bean flour. Later in the morning, his two daughters, Oulchogonime and Ouichil, arrived bringing a big basket of wild strawberries and peaches that are even better than those we had in France.

"You might be curious to know about the appearance of these Indians. I am intrigued with the designs that the Acolappissas tatoo all over their bodies. They prick themselves with needles and rub fine willow ash into their punc-

tured skin. Even their faces are tatooed in this fashion!"
Dr. Dominique glanced at the astonished boys.

Richard said, "Don't stop—keep on reading!"

Dr. Dominique replied, "Boys, do you realize what we
have here? A firsthand account of a French settler's en-
counter with the Louisiana Indians. This is fascinating—
really fascinating!"

"Go on, go on," entreated Rob.

Dr. Dominique carefully turned to the next page and said,
"Listen to this—this describes a religious ceremony.

"After breakfast the Indians proceeded to a round temple
in the center of the village. They rubbed their bodies with a
white clay and then prayed in low tones for a quarter of an
hour. At the temple door there are carved wooden likenesses
of birds, and within the temple there are numerous statues
of dragons, snakes and toads, which are kept locked up in
three small chests. I do not yet understand the significance
of these strange idols. That afternoon I had the pleasure to
accompany the Indians on a hunting expedition. We dressed
in deerskin with the heads and antlers attached and im-
itated the moves that a deer makes. I felt quite awkward and
clumsy but it was amazing to watch the Indians in their
quick deerlike moves. The motion of the disguised hunters
causes the deer to charge, bringing it in closer range for an
easy kill. With this method the Indians kill a great number
of deer.

"At the end of the day, I sat by the fire and taught French
to my host. It was quite comical hearing him pronounce our
beautiful language in his low guttural tones. But it was
probably just as humorous for him to hear me struggle with
his unfamiliar language. Perhaps by the time that we leave,
we will master both.

"We expect to be here through the winter and hope by
then that our supplies will reach us. It has been such an

interesting experience – one that I shall never forget. You are always in my thoughts. Your loving son, Pierre Gabriel."

Dr. Dominique carefully folded the letter and placed it back in the envelope. "Boys, this is a very rare, fragile, and valuable document. This will add a lot to our knowledge of the historical Indians of Louisiana."

Richard interrupted, "Dr. Ben, over at the excavation site, we were looking for evidence of prehistoric Indians. What's the difference between prehistoric and historic Indians? I'm confused."

Dr. Dominique replied, "Good question, Richard. When the Europeans arrived, about the time this letter was written, the prehistoric period ended because the Europeans were able to leave written records about the Indians. You see, prehistoric means before written records, and historic means after. These written accounts are called primary sources. We don't need to go dig up this information – we can just read it. You're probably more familiar with the historic Indian tribes like the Caddo, Chitimacha, and Choctaw."

Rob excitedly interjected, "I've heard of the Choctaws! Once my teacher gave us a whole list of places, rivers, and bayous in Louisiana with Indian names."

Dr. Dominique answered, "Right – most of the river names around here, such as the Abita, the Tchefuncte, and the Bogue Falaya, are Choctaw words."

Richard said, "The Indians have been in Louisiana for a long time, Dr. Ben." Dr. Dominique agreed.

Rob said, "Are there any Indians around now?"

"Sure. I'll bet you boys didn't know that there are three Indian reservations in Louisiana now! Maybe a visit to one can be our next trip."

Both boys said, "That would be great!" Rob added, "Maybe we can go to all three!"

Richard lightly touched the letter Dr. Dominique was holding. "Dr. Ben, how do you know this letter isn't a fake?

Why was it in that desk? Was it supposed to be sent to France?"

"Hold on, Richard. Those are all good questions but I don't have the answers. Remember, I am an archaeologist but a historian could tell you more about this letter. We'll get this letter to an archivist who will conserve and study it. But I have a strong hunch that this letter is the real thing. I wouldn't be too surprised if, in the future, you boys read a copy of it in your history books!"

7

Children of the Earth

Chitimacha Indians, Mid-1700s
St. Mary Parish, Charenton

The squishy mud oozed through Kaposha's toes. She gasped as she edged her second foot into the chilly swamp water. Her dog, Ofe, was yapping and circling a cypress knee at the marshy edge, reluctant to follow her into the murky water. Her skirts were tied above her knees and she steadied herself with a pole as she worked her way across the slick bottom. She finally reached a clump of cane and deftly cut several pieces. It was important that they be of the right maturity and size.

When she had gathered what she needed, she made her way back to dry land, fussing at Ofe for not following her into the swamp. Her feet were red and cold. She stamped them on the ground and rubbed them with grasses to wipe off the mud before she put them in her moccasins.

Kaposha saw the sky was darkening and felt the air getting much colder. She heard the roll of distant thunder, and hurried back to her hut. She carefully lay her bundle of cane down, and drew close to the fire to warm her hands. There was much work to do now that winter was coming. Kaposha began by putting a pot of black dye on the fire to heat. She sat down by her fresh cane and, with her teeth,

split it to the right thickness. Many more baskets needed to be made to store their autumn harvest of corn and grain, and the cane still had to be dyed and dried before it was woven.

Kaposha enjoyed the season of frost and ice. She liked the smoky smell of stews bubbling on the indoor fire and the soft touch of rabbit furs and deerskin around her. She liked the closeness that winter brought. This was the time of year her father repaired his fishing nets, and, although she spent many hours holding the nets taut and straight while he mended them, the time they spent together laughing and joking passed by quickly. In the winter, her mother had much more time to spend showing Kaposha beautiful beadwork and teaching her to sew these intricate colorful patterns on her clothes. Kaposha delighted in this coziness that drew family and friends together against the chill.

Her very favorite thing on long winter nights was to sit by the fire and listen to the ancient tribal tales told by the aged Holy Man. Her parents had given her permission to go to the Meeting House that evening to hear him speak, and after a meal of delicious corn stew and dried berries, Kaposha left with her friends. On the way, they had fun breathing in the icy air and pretending to puff smoke from pipes like their elders, and playing with their shadows made long and thin by the sinking sun.

Many children had already gathered and Kaposha and her friends sat with them, waiting eagerly for the arrival of the Holy Man. As he walked in, the children stood quietly in respect. The Holy One's skin was as creased and cracked as the hide of an alligator. His hair was long and white, weighted down with bits of lead to hold his head erect as befitted his noble birth and position. His eyes were black slits, but they radiated such intensity that they alone seemed to tell his tales. No one knew how old he was, but even Kaposha's grandmother could remember sitting at his feet as a child and hearing the tribal parables. His voice was low and raspy and the children leaned forward to catch every word he spoke. The fire crackled and hissed as the old one began with the story the children never tired of hearing.

"Before the beginning of time, my children, there was only water. The Great Spirit in her loving wisdom made fish and shellfish to live and swim in the vast sea. They were fruitful and soon the sea teemed with creatures of every type. This made the Great Spirit very happy, but still she was not satisfied. She then chose Crawfish and commanded him to dive deep into the black bottom of these waters and bring back the mud and red clay that he found there. The Great Spirit took the mud from the crawfish and formed the earth — the mountains, the plains, the forests, and the deserts. She populated the earth with animals and birds of all descriptions. And then, with the red clay, she fashioned man. This first man she called 'Chitimacha,' which means 'Man who is Red.' This first man was the father of our people."

The Holy Man told several other tales of his tribe's history until he became too tired to continue. His younger assistants helped him up and led him to his hut. As they opened the door flap, the chilly night air rushed in.

The children shivered in the cold and ran to their homes. The only light to guide their way was the faint glow of the fires through the palmetto leaves of their huts.

Kaposha wished her parents a good night and snuggled under the warm furs. She slept on the softest doeskin in the belief that she might acquire the grace and loveliness of that animal. She was almost asleep when the screech of an owl pierced the night, jolting her awake. The eerie sound made her tremble with fear. She ducked her head under the covers, squeezed her eyes tightly shut, and hoped the owl would go away.

After falling asleep, she was awakened again by excited cries calling for her father, Chac-tui, the well-respected medicine man of the tribe. In the dim light of the fire

Kaposha could see Chac-tui leave with his leather pouch containing medicinal herbs and powders. She peeked out into the dark, and saw a large group gathered at the Holy Man's hut.

Her mother came up behind her, put her arm gently around Kaposha's shoulder, and whispered that her father had gone to care for the Holy Man. Kaposha was surprised to see a tear trickling down her mother's cheek. She, too, had heard the owl's cries, and explained this omen of death to Kaposha.

Even at morning the sky remained gloomy and gray. A fine mist shrouded the village. The rain-soaked moss dripped in a slow rhythm. There was no news from Chac-tui, and Kaposha wondered what was taking so long. More hours passed before her father arrived, looking tired and drawn. His head was lowered as he quietly told them that the Holy Man had been called from this earth. Even in his exhausted state, he had to prepare for the funeral ceremony.

The ritual was held in the Village Dance House. Kaposha's father and the other medicine men dressed in special garments. They adorned their bodies with red, black, and white paint and stuck feathers in their long hair. Musicians assembled with drums, gourds, and instruments made from alligator skins and began beating a slow, mournful rhythm. The women wailed in high, keening voices as the body of the Holy Man was carried into the Dance House. The dancing went on for hours and hours. As the women and children waited in the chill air, they could hear the music speed up and the men dancing faster and faster. Then, the drums abruptly stopped and there was a hush as the men emerged from the Dance House and walked in a slow procession to the burial place.

Kaposha was wearied and very cold. She hurried back to her fire and stared at the dancing flames. Her dog, Ofe, laid his head on her knees and whimpered softly. She patted him on his head and hugged him closer to her. She was sad thinking about how much she would miss the revered old man and his wonderful stories. She studied the fire for a long time wondering about that day's events.

When her father returned, Kaposha ran to him to be comforted. He took her onto his lap and listened to her questions. He nodded knowingly and told her that the Great Spirit alone had the answers she wanted, but that she should not be sad about the Holy One, for it was his time to become one with the Great Spirit. Chac-tui said that another holy man would soon continue the stories of their people, and that the Great Spirit would forever protect and guard over their tribe, for they were the children of her creation, they were the children of Mother Earth.

8

Crossed Trails

Caddo Indians, Late 1700s
Caddo Parish

Komiko furtively licked the tip of his finger and dipped it into the sparkly white crystals. "U-m-m!" he crooned as he savored the salty taste. "Komiko! Come!" Komiko hurriedly piled up three of the heavy pottery salt pans and brought them over to the women. Several weeks ago they had filled the pans with water from the saltwater streams, then set them out for the water to evaporate in the glaring summer sun. When all the water was gone and the salt was thoroughly dry, the women took a short stiff brush made from pine needles and brushed the salt into smooth deer hides. They rolled the hides into a funnel shape and slid the salt into narrow-necked clay pots. Salt was used to flavor and preserve food, and most important for Komiko's tribe, it was a trade item. After Komiko had finished carrying all the salt trays to the women, he ran past his village to the grassy plain where the horses grazed.

Although Komiko helped with the salt, his favorite job was tending the horses. He fed them special grains and kept their coats smooth and glossy. When the horses saw Komiko, they trotted to meet him as they nickered a greeting. Komiko rubbed their velvety noses and brushed the tangles from

their long manes and tails. The sun started to set and Komiko took a deep breath of the fresh evening air. He hopped on the back of a horse for a long ride at dusk. When he reached a grassy clearing, he grabbed the horse's mane, squeezed his knees tightly against its body, and raced off in an exhilarating gallop. The wind sang in his ears and his cheeks stung as his hair whipped around his face.

It was almost dark when Komiko slowed his horse to a trot and returned home. He jumped off the horse and walked into his hut. He was surprised to see his uncle, Mako, waiting for him. Komiko was very proud of his uncle. Mako, a tall, strong man, had a shell spike thrust through his nose and had bird and flower tatoos all over his body. He wore a finely polished conch shell pendant engraved with a winged serpent, which was his totem. Mako said, "Komiko, we are going to meet with the white man and exchange goods. Come with us and learn the ways of trade." Komiko was very excited to be included in this select group! They would be bringing horses to trade, along with the precious salt.

Komiko helped the men get ready for the short trip. When they arrived, they camped in the woods outside the stockade fence of the new village. Komiko had never seen a white man before, but his uncle had taught him the special language that was used by many Indian tribes and the new settlers so that all could communicate.

Komiko was so excited he could hardly sleep! When the sun came up and the earth was bright with its light, Mako left to alert the settlers while Komiko and the men readied the trade goods. When Mako and the Frenchmen emerged from the stockade gate, Komiko could hardly stop staring. He knew this was rude and dropped his eyes, but they kept flying back to those strange faces. The men were pale and wan, but they were not sick. Two of the men had hair all around their faces! Komiko could hardly believe what he was seeing. The Indian men plucked off all facial hair with shell tweezers, so that their skin was smooth and their beautiful tatoos showed. One of the men had such pale eyes that Komiko thought he must be blind. Their whole bodies were tightly clothed in pants, belts, leggings, shirts, and boots— how could they be free to run in the forest, climb the trees, and swim in the streams?

When he recovered from his shock, Komiko listened carefully to what his uncle and the head man were saying. Mako and the head man, Monsieur LaForêt, had met many times. They honored each other's honesty and integrity. Komiko looked with pleasure at the items that the Frenchmen were displaying. His mother and aunts would be so happy to have the beautiful glass beads of many colors. They would work these beads into symbolic designs on their skirts. Komiko looked with envy at the shining knives and axes. On the ground were metal pots that were ugly, but did not break like their beautiful pottery bowls. And finally, there was a rifle, a most prized possession for a hunter and warrior. Komiko's eyes gleamed with anticipation of the joyful shouts that would greet them on their return.

Komiko was so intent on looking at all the goods that he forgot to concentrate on what Mako and M. LaForêt were saying. It was only when he saw Mako and M. LaForêt grip hands and move them up and down that he realized that the trade was over. Then Komiko was startled to see the Frenchman's eyes swing towards him. "*Aha, vous vous appelez Komiko. Je suis enchanté.*" He smiled, held out his hand, then switched back to the trade language that Komiko could understand. "Come with me. We will be honored to have you sit at our table and stay the night with us."

Komiko's mouth flew open and he turned to look up at his uncle. What words had he missed while he was dreamily looking at knives, beads, and bells?! Mako sensed Komiko's dismay and explained that M. LaForêt had a son who was the same age as Komiko, and Komiko was invited to their home while the Indians camped outside. Komiko wanted to run wildly back into the woods, but he dared not show his fear to his uncle. What had he gotten himself into, Komiko thought worriedly. But, M. LaForêt smiled encouragingly at him and Komiko followed the Frenchman.

The two walked up to the square house that was made of roughhewn logs. M. LaForêt called out something and a woman walked into the room. "*Mon Dieu!*" cried the startled woman as she saw the strange young boy with her husband, who quickly said something to her. She smiled sweetly and said, "*Bonjour*, Komiko." Komiko noticed that Madame LaForêt was even paler than the men. Her hair was the color of corn silk, and her eyes were the blue of the sky. When Madame spoke, her voice rose and fell like the sound of a rippling stream.

Then she called out, "François, François, *vite! Vite!*" A young boy bounced into the room and stopped abruptly with a look of utter surprise on his face. François held out his hand and Komiko now knew to take it and move it up and down. The French boy smiled delightedly at Komiko, who managed a weak grin. François motioned to Komiko and the two boys walked out together to a large pine tree that had a piece of red fabric nailed to it. François pulled a slender silver object out of his pocket. Komiko watched in amazement as the white boy unfolded a knife that flashed in the sunlight. "*Voilà!*" François held the tip of the knife and spun it toward the target. The knife did not hit squarely and fell to the ground. "*Ah, quel dommage!*" François retrieved the knife and hit the target with a sound thud. "*Bon!*" He pulled the knife out of the tree and gave it to Komiko.

Komiko had never thrown such a knife, and on his first try the flat of the knife hit the tree, so François demonstrated again. After several tries, Komiko was able to hit the target regularly. He found a stick and broke it into equal lengths and showed François how they could keep score. The boys were having a fine time when Madame called out, "Komiko, François, *c'est le temps pour le dîner.*"

François ran to a rain barrel and washed his face and hands, and Komiko watched and did the same. When the boys walked into the room Monsieur and Madame LaForêt were already seated at the rough-sawn table. Komiko was surprised to see Madame because the Indian women always ate separately from the men. The table was covered with a cloth and there was a plate at each place. Komiko did not know what to do and watched the others carefully. M. LaForêt drew his fingers together on his right hand and solemnly touched his forehead, his heart, his left shoulder, and his right shoulder. Was this the same gesture that Mako performed at the beginning of a big feast when he offered the smoke of the sacred peace pipe to the four directions?

After Monsieur finished his ritual, the three LaForêts chanted and Komiko lowered his eyes respectfully. Then Madame filled their plates from large vessels that were on the table. Komiko looked at the objects set by his plate. There was a blunt knife, another utensil with three spikes, and a spoon. He was familiar with a spoon but his were made of buffalo horn or mussel shell. Komiko watched in surprise as the LaForêts picked up the spiked object, speared a piece of rabbit, and plunged it deep into their mouths. Did they stab their tongues? How could he ever manage this?! He picked up the utensil and jabbed a piece of rabbit stew, and carefully placed it in his mouth. It was salty, and also flavored with unfamiliar herbs and spices.

He decided to try some of the other food that was on his plate. There was something green that he could hardly swallow. Komiko pushed his food around and searched for the corn. How could they have such a feast without corn? He took some bread and Madame handed him a bowl with something red and shimmering in it. He put it on his bread, took a tiny bite, then a big one. It was wonderful! Komiko's aunt made a delicious jelly from powdered smilax root, but this was even better. He ate three more pieces of the bread and the shimmering sauce.

When dinner was over, everyone left the table at the same time. In Komiko's village, a big pot of food was cooked in the morning and the people ate whenever they wished. As dusk began to fall, the boys went outside to play a game of hide-and-go-seek. This was fun! Komiko was happy that he had stayed with his new friend. They were running around and playing when Madame called them in again. They climbed up a log ladder to François's small loft. His bed was raised up on four posts, higher than a flea could jump. On the bed was a long cushion stuffed with moss. Komiko's family slept on platforms that were used for benches and tables during the day. Komiko's eyes widened when he saw a shelf with many tiny horses. Seated on each horse was a little man. The horses and men were in different positions, and some of the men were dressed in red and some in blue. He wondered if these were François's totems.

Komiko noticed that François had changed into a looser garment. Madame came in and said, "*Bonne nuit, mes petits garçons*," and blew out the candle. Komiko climbed onto the moss mattress, but did not feel sleepy. He wondered if the white man did everything at a special time. When Komiko was hungry, he ate; when he was tired, he slept. The white people lived in a very strange way!

When the sun shed its first light, Komiko heard Madame walking around and he could smell food cooking. François woke up and got dressed, and the two boys went back to the rain barrel and washed up. As before, everyone sat at the table and chanted. Madame served different breads, and something hot and steaming in small bowls. Komiko was not hungry after his huge meal the night before, but he felt he must show gratitude and ate. It was good, but so different, and he longed for corn cakes and dried buffalo meat.

There was a slight tap on the door, and Mako walked in. He was holding something in a cotton blanket. He spoke to Monsieur, who nodded and smiled at François. Mako handed the blanket and its contents to the French boy. "*Pour moi?*" François was thrilled when he saw the beautiful bow and arrows. "*Oh, merci, merci beaucoup!*" As Komiko turned to leave, François said, "*Un moment, s'il vous plaît,*" and gestured for them to stay. François returned with a tiny horse and handed it to the Indian boy. Komiko couldn't believe it was his to keep! François was truly a fine friend.

On their way back to the village, Komiko kept thinking about his adventure. How different his life was from François's. Komiko was happy to be returning to his own home, to his life of freedom, and to the gift to grow and thrive to the beat of his own rhythm. And one day he hoped that François could visit him at his village, and learn the ways of his people.

9

The Waters of Life

Choctaw Indians, Early 1800s
St. Tammany Parish, Abita Springs

Winona winced as she combed the tangles out of her glistening wet hair. She had just finished a cool, refreshing swim floating in the river's current. As she rested on the sandy beach, she thought of her mother, Tassa. Winona had known that it was almost time for Tassa's baby to be born. Her mother's stomach was so large that it was impossible to climb upon her lap for a squeeze and a hug. Earlier, as the night faded into morning, Tassa told her husband and daughter that the time had come. As was her tribe's custom, a woman was left alone until her baby was born. Winona and her father left their thatched home and walked into the pale spring sunlight. Her father would eat no food and drink no water until sunset. While her father fasted, Winona waited and waited.

She moved over to a sun-warmed log and dried and brushed her hair until it was as bright and shiny as a robin's eye. As she gazed at her wavering image in the dark, sweet water, Winona imagined that she was the Indian girl, Abita, who lived long ago.

Legend held that Abita was the most beautiful maiden in all the land. During the time that Louisiana was under

Spanish rule, a young explorer named Henriquez visited Abita's people and was welcomed at her father's lodge. Her beauty and grace entranced him, and she fell in love with this gentle man. With her father's blessings, the young people were married. Never was a bride more beautiful. She was dressed in her tribal wedding gown, which was of deepest scarlet and purest white.

Henriquez brought his beloved wife to New Orleans, where she was introduced to customs and ideas that were far different from what she knew in her forest home. To please her husband, she tried very hard to learn his ways. But it was difficult to learn Spanish and French as well as the duties that were expected of the wife of such an important man.

As a result, her creamy skin lost its healthy glow, and she became weak and very ill. Her husband was worried, and not even the finest doctors could find the cause of her illness. In desperation, the young Spaniard sought the advice of a healer from Abita's tribe. The advice frightened him, but he felt that there was no other remedy. The wise old medicine man commanded Henriquez to carry Abita deep into the forest to a glen where a stream rippled nearby. He was instructed to leave her for one moon. The healer emphasized that her death would be assured if Henriquez returned before the month had passed. The couple embraced as if for the last time and Henriquez left with deep foreboding and a heavy heart.

The month dragged on and on, until the day finally arrived when he could return. Henriquez reached the glen, but found only the dark ancient cypress trees dripping with gray moss. There was no sign of Abita. He cried out in despair, and to his overwhelming joy, she appeared. She was as healthy and lovely as she had once been, restored by the healing vapors of the stream, as the wise old man had hoped.

All the Indians of the tribe rejoiced, and forever after called these healing springs, "Abita."

Winona's daydream was abruptly broken by a call from her father to hurry home. She scurried up the clay riverbank, her long vigil over. She would soon meet her new brother or sister!

Her father took her hand and held it tightly. Together they entered their home. The room was dark and quiet, and in the corner on a rush bed lay Tassa and a beautiful, healthy girl. Winona ran and gave her mother a big hug, and very gently uncurled the baby's tiny fingers. She kissed the soft round toes that were no bigger than the huckleberries that were just appearing on the bush. Her father stood at the doorway looking at his family with great love and pride.

Winona brought a bowl of fresh water and watched Tassa bathe the tiny child. The baby was lovingly wrapped with long pieces of cloth. Winona was startled when the baby first cried. She could not believe that something so small could make such a loud noise. Tassa satisfied her hungry cries by holding the baby close and nursing her to sleep. Tassa gently lowered the infant into the wooden cradle that had been carved by Winona's father when she had been born. A bag of sand was carefully secured on the baby's forehead, for their people believed that a high flat forehead was a sign of beauty and intelligence.

Soon, the time had come when the baby would be introduced and welcomed into the tribe, but first a name had to be chosen. Many names had been discussed, and even Winona suggested her favorites. One of them was "Bird Singer." The birds had sung so sweetly the day the baby was born. They seemed to be welcoming in the spring and her new sister as well.

The soft, silky touch of the baby's arms and shoulders reminded Winona of the fuzzy down on the new, little ducklings. Only a few days ago by the river, Winona watched quietly as the baby ducks emerged from their cracked eggs. She thought "Soft Feather" might be a pretty name too. Or maybe "Pink Petal," for the baby's tender mouth looked so much like the new buds about to burst into color.

It was such a hard decision to make! But, tomorrow was the ceremony and Winona would finally learn her sister's new name.

Winona woke up early; she was too excited to sleep! Her hair was carefully braided and looped on the sides of her head. She hurriedly slipped on her bright red tunic and white ruffled apron that she wore only for special occasions.

Winona could hear the rhythmic beating of the drums summoning the people to gather. The scent of honeysuckle filled the air as she walked with her family from their home and stood within the circle of friends and neighbors. Her family was honored and she was proud. The tribal holy man stepped forward and with a song implored the god Mingo to bless this child and guard over her. Then placing his hands on her little head, he named her "Abita."

10

Song of Nature

Choctaw Indians, Mid-1800s
St. Tammany Parish, Mandeville

Abbé Rouquette's paddle slipped quietly into the cool waters of the bayou. His sturdy dugout canoe skimmed over the surface with each thrust of his strong shoulders. Abbé Rouquette, a priest, was returning to his nook, a tiny log cabin nestled under the sprawling arms of a huge oak tree.

He had come here to teach the Choctaw, he remembered, and smiled. Things had certainly turned out differently, but then his whole life had been full of surprises. This was surely not the life his parents had dreamed for their son, Adrien. He had grown up in a beautiful mansion in New Orleans and was expected to assume the manners and charm of a sophisticated Creole aristocrat. When he was older, he had sailed to Paris and studied law. But law bored him, and soon Adrien sold his dusty law books and restlessly searched for meaning in his life.

He finally found happiness and peace in the church and quickly won fame for his brilliant sermons. He preached in the finest churches in all of New Orleans, yet his restlessness soon returned. His days were filled with thoughts of his childhood—carefree days spent on Bayou Lacombe across the lake from the city. Those were golden days spent with

Choctaw Indian boys wandering through pine forests, swimming in the muddy bayou water, and practicing their skills with the bow and arrow. These thoughts had inspired him and he decided to help these neglected people.

And so, in a way, his life had come full circle. He was once again in the forest with his Choctaw friends. He had come to bring knowledge and truth to the Choctaw. But instead of changing the Indians, they had changed him. He soon realized that these free people did not need schools that would confine them, or rules that would restrict them. Their classroom was the world of nature and it was in this world that Abbé Rouquette had learned many lessons. He learned to dress as an Indian in deerskin and moccasins. He ate berries, sagamité, and game. He resembled an Indian with his long dark hair and luminous black eyes; now he thought like an Indian as well. The Indians considered him one of their own and called him "Chahta-Ima," which means "like a Choctaw."

A bible verse came to Abbé Rouquette's mind: "There is a time to be born, a time to die, a time to weep, a time to laugh, a time of war. . . . " This terrible, terrible time of war, he thought. All of the country had been gripped by the Civil War and its grasping fingers had even reached out and touched his beloved Choctaw in their remote woods. The scum of both the North and the South had stalked the woods and ravaged the Indians' peaceful community. Their crops were destroyed, their homes and boats battered, and the Indians themselves were driven deep into the swamp. From their hiding places, the Indians would find Abbé Rouquette and ask for food and medicine. It was up to him to keep his people alive.

He turned the boat and beached it, and the bow scrunched on the sand. His Indian friend, Mont-ho-he, silently appeared out of the woods and the two men greeted each other warmly in Choctaw. Others came to unload the heavy bags of dried beans and then one spoke: "Chahta-Ima," said Kateri, "my daughter, Bird Song, wants to see you. She is sick with the swamp fever. My tea of leaves has cooled her fever, but it returns." Chahta-Ima sighed. Many Indians had died from this illness during their exile in the swamp. He quickly gathered his medical supplies from his cabin and he and Mont-ho-he followed Kateri to a small palmetto hut.

Bird Song was a beautiful child with glittering black eyes and glistening hair. She was kind and sweet, and much loved by the Indians. "Chahta-Ima, Chahta-Ima," said the girl when she saw her friend walking through the small opening. Chahta-Ima stroked her dark hair and noticed that although her eyes still twinkled, and she was smiling, her features looked as though they had been carved out of tallow. "Chahta-Ima, please sing my song, the song of the birds that is just for me," she asked.

"Yes, my child, I will sing your song and then you must rest and get well." Chahta-Ima began singing in Creole French, and Bird Song smiled at the funny sounds that she could not understand.

He touched her forehead and walked out with Mont-ho-he, who said, "She is better, Chahta-Ima, but our medicine which makes new blood is low, and she and the other sick ones need more."

Chahta-Ima said, "Then we must cross the Wide Lake, for the city of New Orleans is under seige by the federal government and no more supply boats will be docking on this side of the lake. You must come with me, for I have now passed fifty winters and it is a long and treacherous trip. But we will need a special pirogue."

Mont-ho-he said, "Chahta-Ima, come with me. After our good pirogues were destroyed by the white man's war, my people began to make new boats. One red tree had a very stout pirogue in him. We cut down the tree to get it out, and the boat is almost finished. The men are working on it now

ZOZO MOKEUR

Adrien Rouquette
"Chahta Ima"

tune: Fr. Dominic Braud, O.S.B.

1. Ka- shé dan la barb es- pag- nol ki sa ki a- pé shan- té la? Mo kon- in sé pas ros- sig nol. Kou- té so la voi! Ki si la? La, la. Kou- té so la voi ki si la.

2. Si la, se zo- zo, ki sor- cié. Kou- té, kou- té so la mu- sik. Kou- té li, kou- té li, la pé di nous: "Ki- li- klik! Ki- li- klik!" Klik, klik. Di nous: "Ki- li- klik! Ki- li- klik!" Ah! Mo- keur! Ah! Mo- keur chan- teur! Ah! To gag- nin giab dan kor. To gag- nin tro l'es- prit, mo- keur, mai chan- té! Ma kou- té en- cor.

3. Kou- té li! Shan- gé so la voi. La pé shan- té kom tou zo- zo, kom tou sa ki shan- té dans boi, kom narb, kom de- van, kom do- lo. Lo, lo. Kom narb, kom de- van, kom do- lo.

4. Ga, li dans ciel a- pé val- sé. So la voi a- pé rane li sou, li pli ko- nin sa la pé fé! Li pli ko- nin ar- yin; li fou! Fou, fou, ko- nin ar- yin; li fou! ma kou- té en- cor.

Translation

MOCKINGBIRD SINGER

1. Hidden in the Spanish moss
    Who is that who's singing, there?
   I know it's not a nightingale.
    Listen to his voice! Who is it, there?

2. That's the one, that bird, who is a magician.
    Listen, listen to his music.
   Listen to him—listen to him.
    He's saying to us: "Kiliklik! Kiliklik!"

Chorus

Ah! mockingbird! Ah! mockingbird singer!
    Ah! Ah! You've got the devil in your heart.
You've got too much spirit, mockingbird,
    But sing on! I'll listen again.

3. Listen to him! He's changing his voice.
    He's singing like all the other birds;
   Like everything that sings in the woods:
    Like the trees, like the winds, like the waters.

4. Look, he's waltzing in the sky.
    His own voice is making him drunk.
   He doesn't know what he's doing up there.
    He doesn't know anything anymore—he's crazy!

in the woods near here. Perhaps it is the one to make the trip across the Wide Lake."

Chahta-Ima followed Mont-ho-he to the working site. Small fires were burning in spots on the log not covered by wet mud. Later, scrapers using shells and bones chipped away the charred wood to hollow out the pirogue and to reduce the hull to the desired thickness. The boat would be ready in a few days.

"I will get supplies from my cabin for our trip and will meet you after three suns have set," Chahta-Ima said. "We must cross at night. The Union boats are patrolling Lake Pontchartrain and we will be in danger of being captured if they see us."

On the appointed day, Chahta-Ima arrived at dusk. Mont-ho-he had summoned three strong young companions, Kus, Shulut, and Noslubi, to guide them on their dangerous journey. Before the great war these men had often sailed to New Orleans on small schooners bringing deer, wild turkey, herbs, and a sassafras powder called filé to sell at the French Market. They knew the way well, and could help paddle the sturdy wooden boat.

The men packed smoked dried venison and bags of parched ground corn and pushed the boat into the murky water. The night was bright with stars as they paddled along the shoreline of the lake. Mont-ho-he smiled and pointed to the shining stars above. "What makes you so happy, my friend?" Chahta-Ima asked.

"The stars are spirits of my people who have gone to the heavens. They will watch over us and be our guide. We have no fear."

Chahta-Ima nodded and understood. "My God, who is your Great Spirit, has provided this bright night and calm waters. He holds us in the palm of his hand."

The men paddled for hours on the Wide Lake. They finally reached the familiar waters of Bayou St. John, and hid the pirogue in a remote cove. They had planned carefully. Chahta-Ima put on his scruffiest clothes and, with his long hair, looked like a poor victim of the ravages of war. Mont-ho-he and the others stayed with the boat while Chahta-Ima sought a young doctor, a distant relative, whose home was nearby.

Chahta-Ima made his way to the young doctor's house without attracting any notice. It was noon when he knocked on the door. The servant, assuming he was a beggar in search of food, said kindly, "Go to the back door; the cook will have something for you."

Chahta-Ima protested, "No, I am here to see Dr. D'Anton. I am Abbé Rouquette." The servant knew by his beautifully accented French that this was no beggar. He showed the tattered priest into the drawing room. The servant sum-moned the doctor and told him Abbé Rouquette awaited him. Dr. D'Anton immediately recognized the name, entered the room, and shook Abbé Rouquette's hand enthusiastically. He gave no indication that his clothes were anything but the best.

"Abbé Rouquette! Welcome! I am honored to have you as a guest in my home. I have heard much about you. Is there something I can do?" Abbé Rouquette told him of the need of quinine and other medication. Dr. D'Anton assured Abbé Rouquette he could get these medicines, but it would take several days as he would have to smuggle them out of the hospital under the watchful eyes of the Union guard.

Abbé Rouquette stayed with Dr. D'Anton for three days. He was given fresh clothes, an elegant room, and he dined on the finest foods. But his mind never left his friends in the forest. When enough medicine had been collected, Abbé Rouquette donned his tattered garments, said goodbye to his benefactor, and left to meet with Mont-ho-he.

The trip back was difficult. A strong wind stirred the waters and the waves washed over the sides of the pirogue.

The exhausted men finally reached the Northshore, and welcomed the still bayou. Kateri waited anxiously on the bayou's edge. She was relieved and filled with joy when she saw the boat with its precious cargo of quinine. Mont-ho-he handed her several bottles and she quickly moved through the swamps to distribute the medicine to Bird Song and the sick Indians.

Chahta-Ima's strained muscles burned as he slowly made his way back to his oak tree. Under its spreading arms he knelt, giving thanks to God for their safe return. This tree was his chapel, and his organ and choir were the songs of nature lifted in praise of God. He had heard this from the Indians for they believed that each of God's creations—the wild geese, the crickets, the bayou waters, the trees, the deer, the butterflies, the hummingbirds, and the fish—sang its own song of life, and this living chorus filled the world with glorious harmony. But the Indians' harmonious song with all of nature had been disrupted by the discordant notes of the white man's war. Chahta-Ima wept for his Choctaws, and fell into an exhausted sleep.

The morning bird's sweet song awakened him; the long night's rest had refreshed him and restored his spirit. He knelt once again and was deep in prayer when he was startled by a soft touch on his shoulder. He looked and saw a smiling Bird Song surrounded by Kateri and many other Choctaws. "Chahta-Ima! Chahta-Ima! I am filled with new life!" Chahta-Ima's eyes glistened and he lifted the child so high that her hair brushed the lower branches of the oak.

When he gently put her down, Kateri took Chahta-Ima's hand and said, "We have come to pray with you." Chahta-Ima and the Indians knelt together and their prayers became one harmonious song to God.

11

Child of the Past, Daughter of the Future

Coushatta Indians, Mid-1900s
Allen Parish, Elton

"*Amāpó ihŏchakon sámmit ătato sobáyka bànnampak amasilhǎchit.*"*

"All right, girls," said Mrs. Ellis. "That's not fair. You know I can't understand a word that you're saying!"

"Oh, I'm sorry, Mrs. Ellis. I keep forgetting."

"That's okay, Diana and Shannon," smiled their teacher. "You know that you're really fortunate girls to speak such a rare and complex language. I try, but I don't think I'll ever master your language. Coushatta and English don't even have the same sounds." Diana giggled at the thought of the funny noises her teacher made as she tried to twist her tongue around some of the Coushatta words, such as "fish" and "squirrel."

Mrs. Ellis went on to say, "A unique language can be quite an asset. During World War II, the Navajo Indians, fighting behind enemy lines, used their own language to communicate by radio. The Japanese intercepted these messages, but

---

*"He asked me about it, saying he wanted to know my grandmother's way of life long ago."

couldn't break the 'code.' They must have been really frustrated."

Diana loved languages, and had a real gift for learning them. Her grandmother was very proud of this ability, and called Diana "my little mockingbird" because she was such a natural mimic.

The school day ended, and Diana and Shannon chattered happily in Coushatta all the way home. Diana found her mother and grandmother at work in the kitchen. Her mother was stirring a gumbo in a large pot, and her grandmother was sewing a small basket. These wonderful baskets of alligators, armadillos, lizards, and crawfish were all around the house. Each little basket had a tiny lid and Diana loved to discover what was stored in each.

"Grandmother, what are you making?"

Her grandmother replied, "I don't hear you, little mockingbird. Speak Coushatta to me!" Now Diana knew that her grandmother understood and spoke English perfectly well, but this was her way of preserving the precious heritage of their language. Diana also knew that she would do the same to her grandchildren.

After she had been properly addressed, Grandmother, "Āpó," showed her that the basket she was making would soon resemble a turtle. Diana sat by her grandmother's side, and idly picked up some pine needles and braided them together. Āpó gently took one of the pine needles that Diana was toying with. "See the pine needle and notice how the three needles are bound together as one at the top. In ages so far back in time that only its echoes can now be heard, all people were as one. They spoke one language, and shared what they owned and helped one another.

"There were three brothers born among the people at that time, and as they grew into manhood they became jealous of each other. Each desired what the other owned. They broke all taboos and began stealing corn, deerskins, blowguns, and baskets from one another. The chief and the clan leaders soon saw what was happening, and the three brothers and their families and supporters were banished forever from the land. Each brother traveled far, and formed three separate tribes.

"As time went on, their descendants forgot their common language and they began speaking in different tongues. More tribes were separated, and more languages were spoken. Finally, there were so many languages that one person could not understand what the other was saying. They found they could not live without being able to talk to one another. They realized that all must try to learn a little part of each language, and bit by bit they began to understand. The languages were then joined together as I am sewing this basket, a strand from one tongue, a strand from another. Finally, as this basket became whole and was one, all Indian people again spoke one tongue and all tribes came together in peace and harmony."

Diana sighed as she thought about the story. She knew that these stories were meant to instruct her and that they often had hidden meanings.

When Diana grew older and started high school, she enjoyed helping Mrs. Ellis with the younger children. At free time, they would gather around Diana and she would tell them many of the tales that her grandmother had told to her, and at this time she would insist that all speak in Coushatta. One day Mrs. Ellis interrupted a storytelling session. "Diana, may I see you a moment?" Diana was puzzled, but followed the older woman to the hallway. "Diana, you made excellent grades on the tests that your class took last year. I sent your scores to several state universities, and they are all eager to have you as a student!" Diana gasped as many thoughts went through her mind. "Not only that," continued Mrs. Ellis, "but one university has offered you a substantial grant. Your tuition will be paid, plus you'll have money for living expenses."

"But Mrs. Ellis," said Diana in dismay, "I can't do it! I just can't go away. You know that no one from our tribe has ever been to college before."

"Then you shall be the first, Diana, and I hope the first of many. You will be a wonderful example for all the children in the tribe."

That night Diana sat in her quiet room and tried to collect her thoughts. She placed her hands on the windowsill and breathed in the fresh night air. She could hear the crickets and other familiar night sounds. The moon shone brightly, and tipped the needles of the pine tree with silver. She did not want to leave her land, her family, and her friends, but she knew in her heart that Mrs. Ellis was right. She would attend school to study other languages, and to teach others about the Coushatta language as well. Diana would become a symbol of the future while preserving the legacy of the past.

12

Promise of the Sun

Tunica-Biloxi Indians, Late 1900s
Avoyelles Parish, Marksville

Arrows of sunlight shone brightly on his face as Sam looked toward the sky. With outstretched arms he called to the heavens, "As long as there is the sun, there will be an Indian people. We have your promise." From his position high on top of the flattened mound, Sam imagined he was chief of the tribe a thousand years ago, leading his people in a prosperous trade network and huge construction projects. Sam felt a special pride being a Native American, as he preferred to call himself, and on top of the mound, he felt strongly bound to his Indian heritage

But Indian chiefs get hungry, too, and after hours of playing Sam ran home for supper.

"What's to eat, Mom?" Sam called out, slamming the door behind him.

"Your favorite, Sam, meatballs and spaghetti," his mother answered.

Sam smiled and asked mischievously, "Spaghetti for an Indian chief?"

His mother looked at him with a puzzled expression. "What do you mean for an Indian chief? Are we having company?"

"Oh nothing, Mom. I was just being silly, I guess. I'm starved. Let's eat."

Being an Indian was the most important thing in Sam's life. It was more important than playing football after school, more important than the new bike he got for his birthday, and certainly more important than his stack of baseball cards. He was especially fascinated with the Indians who had lived in Marksville, his hometown. He knew all about the great mounds by the river. He had collected dozens of stone points made by the Avoyels Indians, the "people of the rock" who had occupied this same land four hundred years ago. But, it was the Tunica who had settled in the area in the early 1700s who were his beloved people.

After dinner, Sam went to his room to do homework. It was hard to concentrate on his lessons; he kept thinking about the visit he would soon have at his grandfather's. On his last visit Sam found an eagle feather, a sacred and protective symbol treasured by the Tunica. He kept the feather in a shoe box under his bed and often took it out to hold. Each time, he remembered his grandfather's words, "The eagle has protected our people for many generations. May this feather be a sign that you were chosen to lead our future." Sam felt proud and special, but not exactly sure what his grandfather meant.

After school the next day, Sam jumped on his bike and pedaled to his grandfather's frame cabin. His grandfather was old and bent and his face was creased from many hard years of working in the sun, but his spirit was alive and young.

"Sam, come, before it gets too late. We have important things to learn," his grandfather called. "There are nine burial grounds on this Indian land, and we must see each one."

"Why, Grandfather?" Sam asked. "What's the purpose?"

"The purpose," his grandfather emphasized, "is the land. If you are to lead our people, you must know the land, these few acres that are all that is left of the land which was ours. You must let the dirt slip through your fingers. You must know its pungent smell. You must feel the pulse of the earth beneath the soil, the pulse that our ancestors echoed with the beats of their drums. You must visit the sacred burial grounds, for the living and the dead share the land together. You must become one with the land."

"I have a lot to learn, Grandfather. Let's go."

They spent the weekend visiting the holy graves of their ancestors. Sam's grandfather spoke quietly and reverently while explaining many Tunica beliefs and traditions. He told Sam about the sacred things—Fire, North, South, East, West, Up, Down, Thunder, and especially the Sun. Sam learned about the Orphan Boy who, with the eagle's help, saved the tribe from the monster, Tasiwa, who came from the sky to devour the people. He described the sacred rites of the Corn Festival and explained how the animal dances, the Horse Dance, the Coon Dance, and the Chicken Dance, were to honor the animal helpers of the tribe. It was much to learn.

On the last night, his grandfather spread a blanket on the ground and together they lay down to gaze at the sky. They looked for shooting stars and searched for the "whoopers" who were said to pass across the sky from north to south and from east to west, tying the earth and sky together. They spent hours in silence studying the stars in the Milky Way, the path to the upper world, traveled by the dead.

The next morning, Sam returned home. Before he left, his grandfather held him tightly and said, "Remember the promise of the Sun."

Sam replied, "Oh, Grandfather, I'll never forget. You've taught me the promise since I was little. Besides, I have the eagle feather to remind me."

"Ah, that is right, my son. Now get home. Your mother will worry."

Sam's grandfather died in the early summer and was buried on the land. In the tradition of the Tunicas, Sam brought an offering of new corn and placed it near the head of his grave. He remembered his grandfather's telling him that this act connected the living and the dead. A tear slid down his cheek as he placed the bowl down, but he knew his grandfather was safe within the earth, wrapped in the tender care of the land that he loved.

Sam never forgot the eagle feather or the promise of the sun as he grew into a man. When he graduated from school, he moved into his grandfather's wooden cabin on the Indian land. He was touched by the poverty and terrible living conditions of his people. He could not understand how a people who once had had so much, now had so little. Many before him had worked to gain recognition from the government, and Sam joined in this crusade. This recognition would bring help to his needy people.

Sam worked tirelessly for the Indians. He wanted them to have the very best houses, health care, and education. Because of his dedicated hard work, he was elected tribal chairman or chief. And the biggest honor he could ever imagine was to call his people together to announce that at long last, the United States recognized the Tunica and their brothers, the Biloxi Indians, as a tribe.

Now his people received the help they needed to become once again a brave and proud nation. Paved streets soon crisscrossed the reservation. New brick houses with running water and electricity were filled with the squeals and laughter of families. A brand new playground with swings and slides gave delight to the black-haired Indian children. Sam was overjoyed for his people.

But, one day, Sam heard some news which upset him. A local man had discovered another Indian burial ground, had dug up a hundred sacred graves, and had taken the offerings that had been buried with the bodies. The earth had been desecrated and the Indian bones had been violated, all for these pieces of pottery, tools, jewelry, and beads. Sam demanded that these artifacts be returned to the land of his people, but the fight was long and bitter. In the end, though, the tribe was awarded these treasures.

"We must return them to the land," Sam announced at a Tribal Council Meeting. "We must make peace with our ancestors. I have an idea—please listen. Let us build a mound, a temple mound, one like our forefathers built."

Someone in the crowd stood. "That's a good solution, Chairman. We will bury the treasures back into the mound."

"Well, yes and no," Sam replied. "I know that is confusing so let me explain. We will bury again the offerings in the earth, but we will have a door leading to the sacred tomb, a passageway from the living to the dead. We will have a museum within the mound."

There was silence. In the last row, a woman rose and spoke. "Chairman, you have done much for us. Your hard work has given us jobs and homes and education. You have helped build for our future, and now this museum that you speak of will keep our past alive for generations to come. You have made our elders very happy. Thank you."

Sam stood in the quiet room and said, "You are kind to say those words, but it is our ancestors who preserved this heritage for us, and our people will remain great because of the promise from the sun."

Our Native American Heritage

Louisiana Names from Indian Languages

NAME	TRIBE	MEANING
ABITA SPRINGS (Town & Abita River)	Choctaw	Fountain
AMITE (Town, River)	Choctaw	Young
ATCHAFALAYA (Bay, River, Swamp)	Choctaw	Long River
AVOYELLES (Parish)	Natchez	Flint People
BAYOU ADOIS	Caddo	Brushwood
BAYOU BUSHLEY	Choctaw	Cut Off Creek
BAYOU CASTINE	Choctaw	Flea Creek
BAYOU CHICOT (Lake, River, State Park)	Choctaw	Sluggish Creek
BAYOU FUNNY LOUIS	Choctaw	Black Squirrel Creek
BAYOU GOULA (Town)	Choctaw	Creek People

NAME	TRIBE	MEANING
BAYOU TECHE	Choctaw	Snake Creek
BISTINEAU (Lake)	Caddo	Big Foam
BOGALUSA (Town, Creek)	Choctaw	Black Creek
BOGUE CHITTO (River)	Choctaw	Swift River
BOGUE FALAYA (River)	Choctaw	Long Creek
CADDO (Parish, Lake)	Caddo	Real Chief
CALCASIEU (Parish, Lake)	Atakapa	Crying Eagle
CATAHOULA (Parish, Lake)	Choctaw	Beloved Lake
CHACAHOULA (Town)	Choctaw	Beloved Cypresses
CHINCHUBA (Creek)	Choctaw	Alligator
CHIPOLA (Town)	Choctaw	Feast
CHOUPIQUE (Town, Creek)	Choctaw	Filth
COUSHATTA (Town)	Coushatta	We Are Lost
HOUMA (Town)	Choctaw	Red
KEATCHIE (Town)	Caddo	Panther
KISATCHIE (Town, Creek, National Forest)	Choctaw	Canebreak River
MISSISSIPPI (River)	Algonquin	Large River

NAME	TRIBE	MEANING
NATALBANY (River, Town)	Choctaw	Lone Bear
NATCHEZ (Town, Lake)	Chitimacha	Warrior
NATCHITOCHES (Parish, Town)	Caddo	Chestnut Eaters
OPELOUSAS (Town)	Choctaw	Black Legs
OUACHITA (Parish, River)	Choctaw	Silver Water
PLAQUEMINE (Parish, Town, Bayou)	Illinois	Persimmon
PONCHATOULA (Town, Creek)	Choctaw	Spanish Moss
POWHATAN (Town)	Algonquin	At the Falls
SHONGALOO (Town)	Choctaw	Cypress Tree
TALLULAH (Town)	Choctaw	Sounding Bell
TAMMANY (St. Tammany Parish)	Delaware	Delaware Chief's Name
TANGIPAHOA (Parish, River, Town)	Choctaw	Cornstalk Gatherers
TCHEFUNCTE (River)	Choctaw	Chestnut Eaters
TICKFAW (River, Town)	Choctaw	Piney Rest
TIOGA (Town)	Iroquois	At the Forks of the River
TUNICA (Town, Bayou)	Chickasaw	The People
WHISKEY CHITTO (Creek)	Choctaw	Big Cane

Glossary

ABBÉ. Abbot, a priest who is in charge of an abbey.

ANALYSIS. The separation of a whole into parts for study.

ARCHIVIST. A person who is in charge of keeping records.

ATLATL. A stick used as a spear-thrower. It functioned as an extension of the arm, and enabled the user to throw a spear a greater distance.

BARITONE. A low voice pitch.

CALUMET. Peace pipe.

CHAHTA-IMA. "Like a Choctaw," the affectionate name given to Abbé Rouquette by the Choctaws.

CONCH. The shell of a marine mollusk.

CONSERVE. To protect from loss.

DISCORDANT. Having a harsh sound.

ENGRAVE. To cut or carve into a material.

FEMUR. Thighbone.

FILÉ. Dried, ground sassafras leaves used to flavor and thicken gumbo, a hearty soup.

FILLET. A piece of boneless meat or fish.

FLINT KNAPPING. The process of chipping at flint rock in order to shape it into a stone point.

FUNGI. Plants, resembling sponges, that lack green pigment.

GRUEL. A thin porridge.

INCISED. Cut into; carved.

LICHEN. A type of fungus forming a branching growth on rocks or trees.

MAMMOTH. An extinct elephant.

MASTODON. An extinct mammal resembling an elephant.

METICULOUS. Very careful and precise.

MIMIC. One who copies or imitates.

PALMETTO. Small palm having fan-shaped leaves.

PENDANT. An ornament hanging from a necklace.

POTSHERD. A piece of broken pottery.

PRIMARY SOURCE. Firsthand information.

PUNGENT. Having a sharp, biting smell.

QUININE. Medicine made from the bark of a tree, used to treat malaria.

SAGAMITÉ. A type of bread made of ground corn and beans.

SASSAFRAS. A tree whose bark is used for flavoring.

SINEW. Fibrous tissue that connects a muscle to its bone.

SMILAX. A plant that has climbing vines.

TALLOW. A white or yellow hard fat used to make candles.

THATCHED. Covered with a roof of palms or reeds.

TIPI. Also **TEPEE.** A cone-shaped tent of skins or bark.

TRANSLUCENT. Permitting some light to shine through.

TRIPOD. A three-legged structure.

TUBULAR. Shaped like a tube.

VIGIL. A watch during the night.

FRENCH PHRASES

Bon. Good.

Bonjour. Good morning or hello.

Bonne nuit, mes petits garçons. Good night, my little boys.

C'est le temps pour le dîner. It is time for dinner.

Je suis enchanté. I am delighted (to meet you).

Merci, merci beaucoup. Thank you, thank you very much.

Mon Dieu! My God!

Pour moi? For me?

Quel dommage. What a pity.

Un moment, s'il vous plaît. One moment, please.

Vite. Quick.

Voilà! There!

Vous vous appelez Komiko. Your name is Komiko.